RUINS

Jane Eastoe

RUINS

Discover Britain's Wild and Beautiful Places

National Trust

First published in the United Kingdom in 2019 by
National Trust Books
43 Great Ormond Street
London WC1N 3HZ
An imprint of Pavilion Books Company Ltd

ISBN: 9781911358626

A CIP catalogue record for this book is available from the
British Library.

25 24 23 22 21 20 19
10 9 8 7 6 5 4 3 2 1

Reproduction by Rival Colour Ltd, UK
Printed in China

This book can be ordered direct from the publisher at the
website: www.pavilionbooks.com, or try your local bookshop.

PREVIOUS PAGE
Corfe Castle was
built by William
the Conqueror
and famously
defended by
Mary Bankes, her
daughters and
maids, against the
Parliamentarians.

THIS PAGE
Caerphilly Castle
is Britain's first
concentric castle,
with two sets of
walls for enemies
to overcome.

FSC
www.fsc.org
MIX
Paper from
responsible sources
FSC® C016973

CONTENTS

INTRODUCTION

A ruin is like a marker in time: a skeletal remnant of a once-glorious civilisation, a reminder of political conflict or destruction on a grand scale. Ruins highlight the transience of wealth, good fortune and personal tragedies. They stand as cautionary reminders that we have but a brief time on this planet and our personal contribution, with the odd exception, is but ephemeral.

There does not seem to be any form of construction that man will not tamper with, and that goes as far back as Stonehenge (see pages 34–37). Even Neolithic man could not bring himself to leave the positioning of those huge stones alone, subjecting them to regular rearrangements over a thousand-year period.

The urge to 'improve' and update remains the same – our own homes are small-scale examples. The part we play in construction, extension, redesign, restoration and redecoration is transient. All traces of our former occupation are quietly erased as the next person settles in, full of plans for what they will do with the place.

As our requirements evolve, some buildings become redundant and their perceived value is seen only in destructive terms; fittings can be removed and utilised elsewhere, and valuable lead stripped from roofs for resale. Without a roof for protection, a structure will fall into decay in around ten years. Once the walls start to collapse, stone can be quarried for use elsewhere. This is recycling on a grand scale, and given the scant regard generations past had for 'old relics' which no longer served any useful purpose, it is astonishing that any old buildings survived ruination.

In considering ruins, one person stands out as being single-handedly responsible for the ruinous state of more buildings than would seem humanly possible. Fuelled by his desire to marry Anne Boleyn, Henry VIII appointed himself Head of the Church of England and in the name of reformation set about the dissolution of the monasteries, pocketing their lands, incomes and valuables in the process. Some 800 religious institutions were closed in this single revolutionary act. He has a lot to answer for!

The Romantic and Picturesque movements, which sprung up towards the end of the 18th century, marked a change in mood, in part a response to the brutal impact of industrialisation on the landscape. The two movements emphasised emotion as a source of aesthetic experience, and celebrated a return to nature and an escape from urban life. Key figures in the British movement were the poets William Wordsworth, Samuel Taylor Coleridge, Percy Bysshe Shelley, Lord Byron and John Keats. Wordsworth's 'Lines written a few miles above Tintern Abbey', from *Lyrical Ballads*, was inspired by a visit to Wye in July 1797 and became hugely influential in the veneration of the ruin. J. M. W. Turner and John Constable toured the country in search of charmingly decayed castles and abbeys, driving an appetite for a trend that has become known as 'ruin lust'.

The great and the good initially indulged this passion by pottering around Europe to wonder at an assortment of classical ruins, while happily turning a blind eye to their neglect on the home front. However, the French Revolution limited opportunities for foreign travel and the leisured classes were forced to explore closer to home. Tintern Abbey (see pages 114–117) was the first site to benefit from this new trend.

The passion for ruins became so intense that the wealthy constructed ruined follies – buildings with no function or purpose – to enhance the vistas on their estates aesthetically.

LEFT The view from the engine house at Botallack Mine, Cornwall.

The 18th-century banker Sir Charles Duncombe went so far as to purchase Rievaulx Abbey so that he could tinker with the world-class view from his garden.

In 1871 the Liberal MP John Lubbock, later 1st Baron Avebury, purchased land at Avebury to prevent proposed building works on part of the ancient stone circle; this and other threats to the nation's heritage convinced him that our ancient sites needed proper legal protection. In 1874 he introduced a bill that would identify a list of ancient sites requiring protection; the Ancient Monuments Act came into law in 1882. From this time the Office of Works began to amass a collection of buildings and sites that told the story of Britain.

In March 1877 the textile designer William Morris and architect Philip Webb founded the Society for the Protection of Ancient Buildings. Morris was an early conservationist who fought for 'protection' in place of 'restoration', which he described as a 'feeble and lifeless forgery'. He proposed that ancient buildings should be repaired, not restored so that their entire history would be preserved. The National Trust was formed in July 1894 to prevent the loss of our historic buildings and to protect the natural environment.

By the turn of the century, legislation was further extended to include a wider range of properties and made it a criminal offence to cause damage to them. For the first time national and local governments were empowered to protect buildings of national interest, even those in private ownership. George Curzon, 1st Marquess Curzon of Kedleston, who sponsored the final bill, successfully fought to save Tattershall Castle in Lincolnshire from destruction, and in 1917 purchased and extensively restored 14th-century Bodiam Castle in East Sussex (see pages 48–51), which he later bequeathed to the National Trust. By 1931 some 3,000 monuments had been listed, and 200 taken into public ownership.

Despite the terrible devastation of the Second World War, the movement continued apace. UNESCO (the United Nations Educational, Scientific and Cultural Organisation) was formed in 1945, though the roots of its inception date back to 1922. The United Kingdom currently has 32 UNESCO-listed sites, which range from Stonehenge, Avebury and Associated Sites to the Cornwall and West Devon Mining Sites. The Office of Works' heritage property portfolio continued to grow, and in 1983 a new body, English Heritage, was formed to manage this collection.

As our passion for preserving the remains of our national heritage gained force, it expanded to include our decaying industrial past – the slate mines and gold mines of Wales and the tin and copper mines of Cornwall. Every ruin has a story to tell, of its rise and fall, and of its deliverance from total collapse, picturesque emblems from the past that serve as modern-day morality tales.

The preservation of the United Kingdom's heritage sites remains in all our hands, for what is secure now may not be in the future. In 2015 English Heritage was given charitable status, with the British government gradually withdrawing financial support for the conservation of England's heritage by 2023. The protection of the charity's smaller, more insignificant sites will be dependent on the continuing draw of the big-name crowd pleasers, such as Stonehenge, in funding the repairs backlog. The entrance fee at every ruin you visit, whoever is caring for it, goes some way to supporting the others and to funding repairs to those buildings still on the at-risk register. Use them or lose them.

- SOUTH WEST
- SOUTH EAST AND EAST
- MIDLANDS AND THE NORTH
- WALES
- NORTHERN IRELAND
- SCOTLAND

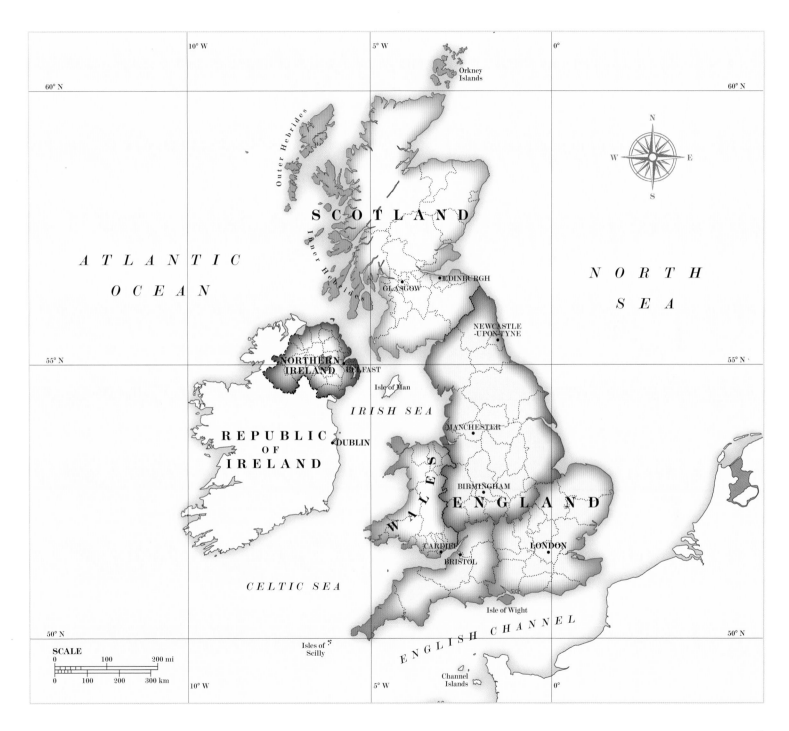

60° N

55° N

50° N

10° W 5° W 0°

**Orkney
Islands**

Outer Hebrides

S C O T L A N D

Inner Hebrides

GLASGOW •EDINBURGH

NEWCASTLE
-UPON-TYNE

**NORTHERN
IRELAND** BELFAST

Isle of Man

**REPUBLIC
OF
IRELAND** •DUBLIN

IRISH SEA

MANCHESTER

W A L E S

BIRMINGHAM

E N G L A N D

CARDIFF LONDON
BRISTOL

CELTIC SEA

Isle of Wight

ENGLISH CHANNEL

Isles of
Scilly

Channel
Islands

*A T L A N T I C
O C E A N*

*N O R T H
S E A*

N

W E

S

SCALE
0 100 200 mi
0 100 200 300 km

SOUTH WEST

SOUTH WEST

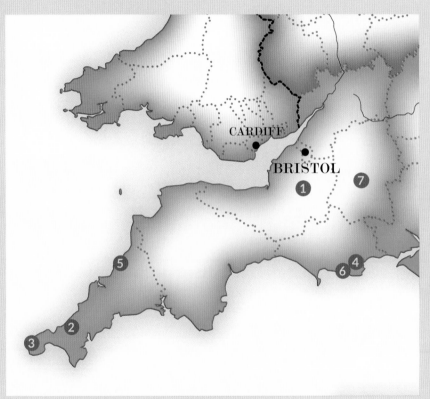

PREVIOUS PAGE
The ruins of Wheal Edward and Wheal Owles at Botallack Mine, Cornwall.

LEFT The outer bailey at Corfe Castle, Dorset.

Myths and legends abound in the South West, so it is perhaps not surprising that so many of its ruins are linked to heroic tales of Arthur, Guinevere and Merlin. Tintagel Castle (see pages 28–31) was constructed by Richard II in the firm belief that it was the place of conception of both Arthur and the Cornish knight Tristan. The monks at Glastonbury Abbey (see pages 14–17) used a similar ploy in the 12th century when funds were low, conveniently uncovering the graves of Arthur and Guinevere in a bid to attract pilgrims. Mighty Stonehenge (see pages 34–37) remains the most mysterious ruin of all. Although excavations have revealed fascinating snippets of information, we still do not understand precisely what motivated this phenomenal exercise in construction.

The west coast of Cornwall was once one of the most important mining areas in the world, but even the harsh realities of day-to-day life here were transformed into escapist fantasy when Winston Graham's Poldark novels related the highs and lows of tin and copper mining. When the industry collapsed, it left behind a landscape scarred with mine workings and punctuated with engine houses as can be seen at Botallack Mine (see pages 22–23). Situated so far from the southern power bases, this diverse range of man-made edifices came perilously close to total ruin and destruction through wanton neglect.

GLASTONBURY ABBEY

The Dissolution of the Monasteries by Henry VIII (1536–41) saw the closure of over 800 religious institutions. Most were given up without incident, but what took place at Glastonbury Abbey in Somerset, one of the oldest and wealthiest religious institutions, was to serve as a cautionary tale, a public signal of the extent of the King's power and ruthlessness.

Richard Whiting (1461–1539), Abbot of Glastonbury, was described by Cardinal Wolsey as: 'An upright and religious monk, a provident and discreet man, a priest commendable for his life, virtues and learning'. Realising he had little option, Whiting had the good sense to sign Act of Supremacy in 1534, accepting Henry as head of the Church of England. When Thomas Cromwell dispatched commissioners to Glastonbury to inspect their accounts in 1535, no fault could be found, despite their efforts to the contrary.

Richard Layton, Henry VIII's most ruthless commissioner, was dispatched on a second visit four years later. The Abbot had the misfortune to be elsewhere on business when Layton arrived, and returned to find the Abbey being plundered and his personal rooms ransacked. The King's man claimed to have found money in the Abbot's chambers which he took to be a clear signal of financial wrongdoing. Worse still, Layton maintained that the Abbot was in possession of a document decrying the king's divorce from Catherine of Aragon.

The 80-year-old Whiting was taken to the Tower of London for questioning, then returned to Glastonbury for trial with a note that read: 'Abbot of Glaston to be tried and executed there with his accomplices.' The trial,

LEFT Lady Chapel at Glastonbury Abbey. Enough of the Abbey walls remain to give a sense of scale.

which should have been held by his peers in the House of Lords, was a mere formality and the guilty verdict had been decided in advance.

The Abbot and two of his monks, John Thorne and Roger James, were dragged on hurdles through the streets of Glastonbury to the top of Tor. Here they were hung, drawn and quartered. Whiting's head was fastened over the west gate of the Abbey, and as further indignity, his quarters were boiled in pitch and displayed in Bath, Ilchester and Bridgewater. The Abbey was stripped, its tombs destroyed, and the long working life of this revered institution ended.

The date of the earliest church at Glastonbury is a matter of some speculation. Legend has it that Joseph of Arimathea constructed the first church here shortly after the death of Christ.

Archaeological research using radiocarbon dating has confirmed that shards of pottery from the site date from around AD450–550. This indicates that Glastonbury was occupied by Romans and Saxons in the 5th or 6th centuries, well before the confirmed founding of the first monastery.

The earliest recorded church on the site was constructed around AD720 on the orders of the Anglo-Saxon King Ina (or Ine) of Wessex, who ruled from AD688–726. This new stone church almost certainly replaced an existing timber church, so the institution can reasonably claim to be even older than this. Ina's church was ravaged by the Danes in the 9th century, and when Dunstan (909–988) became Abbott in 943 he restored and enlarge the ruined abbey and established Benedictine rule. Over the next century each abbot seemed hell-bent on bettering the work of the last, and there was much knocking down and rebuilding work to occupy the monks. Records from the Domesday Book of 1086 reveal that Glastonbury was the richest of England's abbeys.

In 1184 a fire devastated the Abbey, necessitating a complete rebuild. It also conveniently destroyed all the Abbey's records, giving the monks licence to embellish Glastonbury's history. They deliberately utilised an archaic architectural style in the reconstruction to emphasise the Abbey's ancient pedigree, even though it was in effect brand new. On the orders of Henry II, the Lady Chapel was the first to be rebuilt and remains one of the best-preserved sections of the ruins. The graves of King Arthur and Queen Guinevere were conveniently uncovered in 1191 when funds for rebuilding were running low.

Between the fire in 1184 and the dissolution of 1539, the church was continually extended and improved, the precinct was redefined, a new house was constructed for the Abbot, and a specially-designed octagonal kitchen was built to cater to the culinary needs of the monks. This alone survived the dissolution and the ravages of time unscathed, possibly because it was used as a Quaker Meeting House.

By the 18th century Glastonbury Abbey was described as a ruin. It was still being plundered for stone as late as the early 19th century. In 1882 the Ancient Monuments Protection Act was passed, and the site protected from further damage. In 1908 the Abbey ruins were purchased by the Church of England and it remains under its guardianship.

RIGHT The ornate floor tiles show that the Abbey was once colourful and luxurious.

FAR RIGHT The walls at Glastonbury Abbey would have been painted and gilded.

EAST POOL MINE, CORNWALL

Mining in Cornwall can be traced in some form back to the Bronze age, but it began in earnest in the 16th century. It continued through boom and bust until the 1930s, although the last tin mine, South Crofty near Camborne, remained open until 1998. The county was the biggest producer of copper until the 1860s, when tin became a more profitable commodity. But, behind the fortunes that could be made, was the grim reality of what extracting tin and copper from the ground actually entailed.

Pool Old Bal, as the mine was first known, opened in the early 18th century and operated until 1784. When work resumed in 1834 it was renamed East Pool Mine. At its peak almost 300 people were employed, with half working above ground, and half below ground. Most of the work above ground was done by girls and women known as 'bal maidens' ('bal' means 'mine'), who broke up the ore by hand before it was loaded onto trolleys to go for further processing. Boys as young as 13 were sent underground with the men.

Miners descended by a series of ladders, with deeper mines sometimes dropping over 300m (1,000ft), reached by lift-like cages. The miners worked eight-hour shifts, six days a week and would relieve themselves underground in winzes (small ventilation shafts) when the need arose, making them vulnerable to disease.

LEFT Mitchell's Engine House at East Pool Mine.

RIGHT Work 'at grass', or above ground, was as important a part of the mining operation as the underground workings.

Other common illnesses were tuberculosis, silicosis, bronchitis and rheumatism. Rockfalls, flooding and blasting accidents were other dangers. The tunnels were incredibly hot and airless, and the stench was terrible.

However, in the 19th century Cornwall became world famous as a centre for innovation in mining and engineering, and, with the technical advances in machinery, the number of children working in the mines declined. In 1842 the Mines Act was passed, banning women and boys under the age of ten from working underground.

The land within which East Pool was situated was owned by the Basset family, one of Cornwall's largest landowners, who grew wealthy on the proceeds from this and other mines. East Pool Mine alone produced 92,000 tonnes of high-grade copper ore and 47,000 tonnes of tin ore its working lifetime.

The deepest workings at East Pool were 550m (1,800ft), but the ingress of water from other nearby mines, including Wheal Agar was an ongoing problem. Pumping water from the shafts was of the highest priority, and in 1895 Wheal Agar mine followed up its threats to cease pumping and flooded the productive lower levels of East Pool mine. Negotiations between the two companies continued for a year until finally, in 1897, East Pool Mine purchased Wheal Agar Mine and its equipment for £4,000.

In 1921 the East Pool and Agar mine's main shaft collapsed, necessitating three years of work constructing a new shaft, dug some 250m (820ft) from the original one. Dubbed Taylor's Shaft, it was serviced by a pumping engine – among the last of its kind to be produced before the move over to electricity – which pumped water from the mine 24 hours a day. This mine became an important producer of tungsten, which was used for armour plating and in the production of weapons, and much in demand during the Second World War. When the conflict ended, mining subsidies were stopped; East Pool and Agar Mine was no longer profitable and work ceased. Taylor's engine continued to run until September 1954 keeping water out of the neighbouring South Crofty mine, when it was finally replaced with electric pumps.

RIGHT The area of the mine above ground was where the ore was broken up.

BOTALLACK MINE, CORNWALL

A stretch of West Cornwall's rugged Atlantic Coast over 11.3km (7 miles) long is thought to have been the site of mining for over 2,000 years. Tagged the Tin Coast, the ground here is riddled with hundreds of mine shafts, some of which stretch out below the sea, and the land is peppered with ruins that hint at its once-thriving industrial past. Botallack Mine lies within this stretch of land in West Penwith and tin has been extracted here commercially since the 16th century, though there is evidence of earlier medieval steam working.

Mining districts across Cornwall contains percentages of tin, copper, lead, tungsten, arsenic and iron which leached out from cooling magma, via fissures in the granite into faults in the surrounding rock. The ores are mined vertically, unlike coal which is minded horizontally. By the 1830s Cornwall dominated the world production of copper.

Early mineral extraction was undertaken by steam workings and then shallow underground mining. The first steam engines were installed from the mid-18th century, triggering ground breaking changes in the industry. The steam engines pumped water out of the mines, enabling miners to work at greater depths than had previously been possible. This was a boom and bust industry: profits depended on the quality and quantity of minerals that could be uncovered before the mine shaft was exhausted, and on fluctuating trading prices. Botallack opened and closed several times.

The mine shafts at Botallack reached nearly 800m (½ mile) under the sea. Perched on the cliffs above are the towering 'Crowns'; the lower a former pumping engine and the other used to bring men up and down the Boscawen Diagonal Shaft. The Prince and Princess of Wales visited in 1865, descending into the mine to visit a new section. Where royals led, others wanted to follow and descending the shaft at Botallack became something of a tourist attraction. The mine was eventually forced to charge visitors a guinea for the privilege.

In its working lifetime Botallack produced some 14,500 tonnes of tin, 20,000 tonnes of copper and 1,500 tonnes of refined arsenic – the mineral is a lucrative by-product of tin mining and Botallack was home to two arsenic works. As the ore was roasted, gases cooled in the labyrinthine, snaking, horizontal flue, depositing an arsenic residue. Men and small boys were sent into the flue to scrape off and collect the arsenic. With a nod towards health and safety they tied rags around their noses and mouths.

The discovery of metals in North America, Chile, Spain, Australia and Malaya marked the beginning of the demise of the Cornish mining industry. These low-cost workings forced the world price down, the mine was closed and the last men were discharged from the Botallack on 15th February 1896. Despite several attempts at re-working, most recently in 1980, the ore was not deemed to be of good enough quality and quantity to start mining significantly again. The mine came into the care of the National Trust in 1995.

RIGHT A view of the 'Crowns' on the cliffs at Botallack.

CORFE CASTLE, DORSET

orfe Castle stands in an exceptional Dorset location in a gap between the Purbeck Hills. The site was fortified by Saxon Kings, though nothing remains of this castle. In 978 it was the site of the murder of King Edward the Martyr (c.962–978). He was the elder (possibly illegitimate) son of Edgar the Peaceful, but his younger half-brother, Ethelred the Unready (c.966–1016) was recognised as the legitimate heir. Even so, Edward, who was notoriously ill-tempered, would probably have been the obvious first choice for the throne had he not offended so many nobles. Both boys were too young to play a major role in the turmoil that followed, but Edward's supporters won the day. He was crowned at the age of just 13 in 975 and murdered three years later at the gates of Corfe Castle, in an attack by his half-brother's supporters while dismounting his horse. He was unceremoniously buried here, but his brother ordered his reinterment at Shaftesbury Abbey a year later.

William the Conqueror (c.1028–87) instigated the building of a new stone castle at Corfe ringed by a timber palisade. This was further fortified by Henry I (c.1068–1135) who ordered the construction of a stone keep, which used Purbeck limestone from a nearby quarry. The work was finished by 1105.

RIGHT Corfe Castle had a long and bloody history.

King John (1166–1216), who a contemporary chronicler described as brim-full of evil qualities, undertook further refortification and used Corfe Castle as a prison and a treasury – he kept his royal regalia here. He imprisoned his 'dearest niece' Eleanor, the Fair Maid of Brittany, to gain control of her lands and stave off any threat to his throne. Twenty-two of her knights were also imprisoned; following a failed escape attempt the King simply allowed them to starve to death. When King John died, he was succeeded by his son Henry III (1207–72) who followed his father's order that Eleanor should never be released. She may have been treated like a royal princess in captivity, but still had to endure 39 years under confinement at Corfe Castle.

Queen Elizabeth I sold Corfe Castle to her Chancellor, Christopher Hatton, who fortified it in readiness for an attack by the Spanish Armada. The Hatton family sold it to Sir John Bankes, Charles I's Lord Chief Justice, in 1635. His wife, Mary, defended the castle alone against the first of two sieges by the Parliamentarians – it was only an act of treachery by one of her own officers that led to its ultimate fall. A vote was later passed in the House of Commons to 'slight' the castle, and gunpowder was used to demolish it.

The ruins of Corfe Castle were returned to the Bankes family with the restoration of the monarchy in 1660. Rather than rebuilding it, Mary's son Ralph opted to commission a new house at Kingston Lacy in Dorset and retained Corfe Castle as a romantic ruin. In 1891 his descendant, Ralph Bankes, bequeathed Corfe Castle, and the house at Kingston Lacy, to the National Trust and it remains under their guardianship.

LEFT The Keep at Corfe Castle.

TINTAGEL CASTLE, CORNWALL

Doubtless Gervase de Tintagel couldn't believe his luck the day that Richard, Earl of Cornwall (1209–72), the second son of King John of England, swapped three manors, including his house of Merthen, in exchange for a small rocky headland in Cornwall. The island of Tintagel was connected to the mainland by a narrow cliff bridge, it had absolutely no strategic value and faced the full, brutal force of the Atlantic elements.

The island appealed to Richard because of its supposed links with Arthurian Legend, as created by Geoffrey of Monmouth in *Historia regum Britanniae* ('History of the Kings of Britain') c.1138. The book relates how Uther Pendragon, the legendary King of pre-Roman Britain, used magic to seduce Igraine, the wife of one of his barons, who subsequently bore his child, Arthur. The book was hugely influential in the development of the Arthurian legend in medieval Britain, but historians have been unable to find a shred of evidence to confirm that this story is anything other than mere legend.

Nevertheless, Richard would have been familiar with the story and would have regarded the ownership of Arthur's place of conception as a means of linking himself with Arthurian myth, and also as a way of strengthening his new position as Lord of Cornwall. Richard funded the construction of a stone castle, a chapel and a garden within a series of defensive wards and used considerable funds to create this status symbol. The inner ward of the castle is perched high on a crag on the island, though it was rather more accessible in the 13th century than now; coastal erosion washed away the neck of the headland in the 15th century. The outer bailey lay on the mainland clifftop; the curtain walls – given the breezy location – were on the flimsy side.

Tintagel has stronger links with the legend of Tristan and Iseult, with which Richard would also have been familiar. Large parts of the story, the origins of which are unknown, are set at Tintagel in the court of King Mark of Cornwall, coincidentally, also Tristan's place of conception. It has been suggested that this, rather than the Arthurian legend, was Richard's inspiration for the design as many details closely replicate descriptive elements of King Mark's castle.

BELOW Tintagel perches beside the Atlantic.

RIGHT Stout walking shoes are recommended to explore the site.

Richard entertained the Welsh Prince Dafydd ap Llywelyn at Tintagel in 1242. Daffyd's loyalty to Henry III, who had stripped him of all his lands outside Gwynedd, was understandably questionable. If it was an attempt to keep Dafydd on side it failed, for Richard later campaigned in Wales against Dafydd on behalf of his brother. Richard had numerous properties, both in Cornwall and elsewhere, and spent little time in his fantasy palace. After his death no one was much interested in Tintagel Castle and it passed to the High Sheriff of Cornwall, who used it as a prison. In the 1330s, the roof was removed from the Great Hall. Edward, the Black Prince (1330–76) was created Duke of Cornwall in 1337 and visited the castle. He commissioned repairs, but never spent any significant time there, and whatever work was undertaken was quickly undone by neglect and the elements.

William of Worcester described the castle as in ruins by 1478, and John Leland, who has been described as the father of local history, visited in the 1540s and found that access to the island was via a makeshift bridge made of tree trunks. By the Victorian era the castle ruins had become something of a tourist attraction. It was protected by the Ancient Monuments Act in 1931 and is now in the care of English Heritage.

LEFT Hardly any of the castle remains, but the views are spectacular.

TYNEHAM VILLAGE, DORSET

In the autumn of 1943 the 252 residents of Tyneham village in Dorset were given one month to leave their homes as part of the war effort. The official communication stated: 'The Government appreciate that this is no small sacrifice which you are asked to make, but they are sure that you will give this further help towards winning the war with a good heart.'

The land on which the village lay was being commandeered by the War Office for military training in the run up to D-Day, although as all plans were cloaked in secrecy no one was aware of this at the time. Nevertheless, the villagers did as they were ordered and abandoned Tyneham, leaving it a ghost village. The valuable church fittings, including the Jacobean pulpit, the bells and the organ, were moved to a nearby church for safekeeping. One forlorn note pinned to the church door read: 'Please treat the church and houses with care; we have given up our homes, where many of us have lived for generations, to help win the war and keep men free. We shall return one day and thank you for treating the village kindly.'

The village, which dated back to the time of William the Conqueror, had been quiet and peaceful; the school had closed in 1932 due to a lack of pupils. The houses had neither electricity nor running water. A phone box had been installed only shortly before the order to evacuate the village came. As soon as the village was cleared, access to it, and to over 3,000ha (7,500 acres) of surrounding land was prohibited. Tyneham House, which had been owned by the Bond family for over 300 years, was used as a billet by the WAAF (Women's Auxiliary Air Force), and the village was subject to bombardment.

The villagers believed Churchill's pledge that they would return, but in 1945 the military maintained that, with the advent of the Cold War, it needed to retain the land for training purposes. In May 1968 the Tyneham Action Group was formed to act on behalf of the villagers who wished to return, but in 1974 a Government White Paper concluded that Tyneham was still required for army training. Its ruins remain off-limits for much of the year.

The Bond family received £30,000 in compensation for their house and land. After the war it was stripped of its contents, which were sold, and it was eventually demolished. Most of the villagers lived in tied cottages and were only compensated for the loss of the vegetables in their gardens. Surviving residents retain the right to be buried in the graveyard at Tyneham if they so wish.

Today the land is still owned by the Ministry of Defence and it remains in use as a military range. The ruins of this tranquil village can be explored on open days; the church and the school house, which have survived intact are preserved as museums.

LEFT The War Office used the land around Tyneham for military training as part of D-Day preparations.

STONEHENGE, WILTSHIRE

On 21 September 1915 an auction was held at the Palace Theatre, Salisbury. Lot 15 was listed by Messrs Knight, Frank and Rutley as: 'Stonehenge with about 30 acres, 2 rods, 37 perches of adjoining downland.' One Cecil Chubb attended the auction, with instructions from his wife to purchase some chairs. He had no intention of bidding for Stonehenge and admitted he put his hand up on impulse, later relating, 'While I was in the room I thought a Salisbury man ought to buy it, and that is how it was done.' Chubb won Lot 15 with a top bid of £6,600. What Mrs Chubb though of the purchase is not recorded, but it is doubtful that she ever allowed her husband near an auction house again.

Cecil Chubb was the last private owner of Stonehenge. Three years after his impulse purchase he gave Stonehenge to the nation on several conditions. These include: that the public should have unrestricted access for a fee; that the site should be maintained in its present condition; and that no buildings other than a pay box should be erected within 400 yards (365m) of the milestone marked 'Amesbury 2'. For this singular act of generosity to his country Lloyd George made Chubb a baronet in 1919.

Stonehenge, in the estate of Amesbury, had been owned by the Crown from the time of King Alfred in 899, but from 1140 onwards it was given out to members of the nobility. Henry VIII gifted it to Edward Seymour, Duke of Somerset, his third wife's brother. From the 17th century it passed through many hands until it was purchased by Edmund Antrobus in 1825.

Stonehenge had been a tourist attraction for centuries, and in 1901 Sir Edmund Antrobus began charging admission to the site. His only son was killed at the Battle of Ypres (1915), just a few months before his own death. With no heir the estate passed to his brother Sir Cecil Antrobus who decided to sell up. That Stonehenge came into public ownership is a matter of chance.

The site has been recorded by scholars since Medieval times. The first known dig at Stonehenge was undertaken in 1620 by George, Duke of Buckingham, a favourite of James I, who had a hole dug in the middle to see what was there. The heads and horns of stags and oxen, charcoal arrowheads, rusty armour and rotten bones were all unearthed.

At one of the round barrows or burial mounds on King Barrow Ridge, a silver-tipped bugle horn was uncovered, a find the Duke shared with James I. The King was so excited that he commissioned the architect Inigo Jones to make a survey of the site. From this time onwards Stonehenge and the surrounding area, which is littered with barrows and home to standing stones at Amesbury, has been subjected to countless archaeological excavations. Yet despite this almost continual activity we still do not understand why Stonehenge was constructed.

Seen from the air, Stonehenge is ringed by a vast circular ditch and within this lies a ring of 56 chalk pits, known as the Aubrey Holes. These were named after the 17th century antiquarian, John Aubrey, who first noted their existence. These pits, now filled with concrete, are the oldest part of Stonehenge and date back to at least 3100 BC. Excavation showed them to have been filled with cremated bones. Experts surmise that the holes may have once supported stones, subsequently removed, or timber poles.

From around 2600BC the bluestones, some weighing as much as four tonnes, were somehow transported from the Preseli Mountains in north Pembrokeshire, Wales, and erected in a circle, though these were repeatedly shuffled around and rearranged in a giant form of interior redecoration.

The next phase of work took place between 2600 and 2400BC when 25-tonne sarsen stones were brought to the site, possibly from a quarry on the Marlborough Downs just over 40km (25 miles) distant as the crow flies, to form a ring of 30 stones. These are topped by dressed and shaped stone lintels, which are linked with an early form of mortise and tenon joints. It is this detail that qualifies Stonehenge to count as a ruin, rather than plain standing stones. The reorganisation of the bluestone circle continued until between 1930 and 1600BC, when the horseshoe pattern was settled on.

When Sir Cecil Chubb gave Stonehenge to the nation in 1918 it was passed into the care of the Commissioners of Works and is now managed by English Heritage. The National Trust owns tracts of land around Stonehenge, and in 1986 the area was UNESCO-listed and dubbed, Stonehenge, Avebury and Associated Sites.

RIGHT The lintels that top the standing stones were dressed and shaped.

FOLLOWING PAGE The perfect layout of the great bluestones was the cause of some dispute amongst Neolithic man, and they were repeatedly rearranged.

SOUTH EAST
AND EAST

SOUTH EAST AND EAST

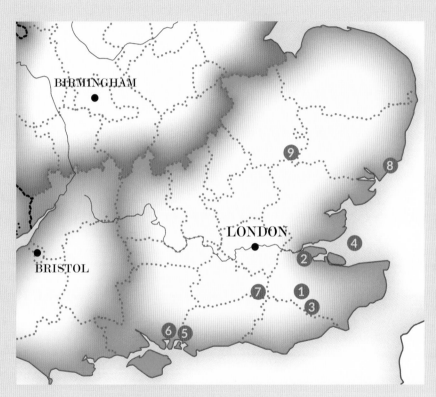

PREVIOUS PAGE
The Pagodas at
Orford Ness where
bomb detonators
were once tested.

LEFT The ruins
of 14th-century
Scotney Castle
in Kent.

Marked less by internal struggles, the ruins of the south east and the east highlight the fight to defend Britain from foreign invasion. Fortifications like Portchester Castle (see pages 56–57), constructed by the Romans and refortified by the Normans, are strung out along the south coast. In the 14th century a series of French raids on the Kent and Sussex coast saw a flurry of applications to the Crown for a licence to crenellate; no one was allowed to fortify their home without royal permission. Bodiam Castle (see pages 48–51) in East Sussex and Scotney Castle (see pages 42–45) in Kent were both constructed to guard against the possibility of such attacks. Defending London was also a priority; towering Rochester Castle (see pages 46–47) was constructed in the 11th century to guard the road between London and the Kent coast. The Maunsell Forts (see pages 52–53) were thrown up in the Thames Estuary to protect the port of London during the Second World War and later served as home to pirate radio stations. Now long abandoned, these great rusting sea sentries highlight the evolution of British military defence, as do the other-worldly ruins of Orford Ness (see pages 62–65). Developed as an armament testing base in the First World War, it was later pressed into use as a base for top-secret experiments in radio direction finding, before evolving into an Atomic Weapons Research Establishment in the Cold War.

SCOTNEY CASTLE, KENT

The ruins of Scotney Castle in Kent are a shining example of the human need to improve, refurbish and rebuild according to contemporary fashion. Records show that this land has been occupied since at least the Domesday Book published in 1086, when it was owned by the Bishop of Bayeux, half-brother of William the Conqueror. It was then acquired by the de Scoteni family who relinquished their ownership in about 1285, though the name was retained. The estate passed through various hands before being acquired by the Ashburnhams in 1358.

It is not known what the original buildings were like, but after attacks by the French on England's South Coast during the Hundred Years' War (1337–1453), notably on Folkestone and Rye in 1377, Roger de Ashburnham, Conservator of the Peace in Kent and Sussex, became nervous and decided it would be judicious to build a fortified manor house – the wisdom of which was doubtless justified following further attacks by the French on Winchelsea in 1377.

Scotney Castle was built on two moated islands formed by diverting a loop in the River Bewl. One island was enclosed by a curtain wall, with four round towers at each corner where a hall provided the main accommodation, while the other island housed service buildings, such as stables. The castle's new defensive structure may have helped Sir Roger sleep a little easier, but it would not have posed much of a challenge to an attacking force; the walls were too low, there were no gunports and the moat could have been drained. Fortunately it was not put to the test.

In c. 1580 the hall was rebuilt by its new incumbents the Darrell family, who incorporated the Elizabethan design. The Darrells were staunch Catholics, and a priest's hole was constructed, later utilised as a hiding place by Father Richard Blount who eventually became the leader of the Jesuits in England. Substantial rebuilding work took place again in the 1630s, and the Darrells remained at Scotney until the mid-18th century when debts forced its sale.

In 1778, Scotney Castle was purchased by Edward Hussey. His grandson, also Edward, made a list of 'objections to the Present House at Scotney', which included the lack of bedrooms – even though he was a bachelor at the time – as well as the cold, damp evenings and an entrance that was bad in wet weather. In November 1834 he met the architect Anthony Salvin, and the 'New Castle' was designed in Tudor revival style and built using sandstone from the estate quarry. The work took some nine years to complete. The landscape designer William Sawrey Gilpin was employed to develop the garden. He incorporated the old castle into his scheme, much of which was dismantled for a picturesque ruined effect, and some of the stone was incorporated into the new building.

Five generations of the Hussey family lived at Scotney – three of them at the new house – and the estate was bequeathed to the National Trust in 1970. The ruins remain in the garden and survive as a cautionary reminder of what happens when the practical needs of the present override the glorious, but less hospitable, buildings of the past.

RIGHT Scotney was a family home until the 1830s.

FOLLOWING PAGE The castle was preserved in ruined form as part of the new garden design.

ROCHESTER CASTLE, KENT

The keep of Rochester Castle has remained defiantly upright for nigh on 900 years, despite being roofless for 400 of them. It has withstood sieges and centuries of neglect, yet miraculously remains virtually unchanged from the original Norman construction. Its position highlights the strategic importance of this location on the main road from London to Canterbury and Dover at a crossing point of the River Medway.

Gundulf, a French monk who came to England to help with the reorganisation of the English monasteries, directed his energies towards the construction of the new Rochester Cathedral when he was first appointed Bishop of Rochester in 1077.

Gundulf oversaw the construction of the stone curtain wall, at his own expense, which incorporated sections of the old Roman city wall. Building of the keep was down to William de Corbeil (c.1070–1136), Archbishop of Canterbury, who was entrusted with the guardianship of Rochester Castle on condition he improved its fortifications. Work began in 1277 on what was to become England's tallest keep measuring 35m (115ft), a shining example of Norman construction and a secure place for the archbishop.

Rochester Castle's most famous siege was in 1215, in a rebellion between King John (1166–1216) and his barons, after the King reneged on Magna Carta. The barons holed up in the castle while the King directed the might of five siege engines at the keep, but its walls were 3.6m (12ft) thick and the assault made no impression. The King's men tunnelled underneath but the wall still held. A fire brought down a section of the curtain wall but the barons retreated behind the dividing wall where

the well was situated and continued to hold out. In total, the rebels were under siege for two months before they surrendered.

Unrest continued until 1216 when King John died of dysentery. His son Henry III (1207–72) succeeded him aged just nine years old and he later oversaw a 20-year period of renovations at Rochester Castle, including rebuilding the keep wall at a curve to better deflect missiles and resist undermining.

The castle came under siege again in the Baron's War of 1264; the curtain wall was breached, and this damage was not repaired for another 100 years when Edward III rebuilt large sections in the 1370s against the threat of a French invasion. Richard II constructed a bastion on the north-east side of the castle and had rebuilding work undertaken after the pilfering of stone. The castle last saw action during the Peasants' Revolt in 1381.

In the 15th century the castle bailey was let to tenants, and in the latter part of the 16th century Elizabeth I gave permission for stone from the curtain wall to be used for the construction of a new artillery fort at Upnor, in nearby Medway, to protect warships moored in the Chatham dockyards. In the 1660s a fire gutted the castle's interior and it fell into disrepair. The ruins quickly became a draw for visitors that included both Samuel Pepys and Charles Dickens. The Corporation of Rochester purchased the site in 1884 and the castle grounds were turned into public pleasure gardens. The Ministry of Works assumed control of the keep in 1965, and it was placed under the guardianship of English Heritage in 1984, although Medway Council manages the keep and the castle gardens.

BODIAM CASTLE, EAST SUSSEX

On first view, Bodiam Castle does not look like a ruin at all. It sits in a vast rectangular moat, just north of the River Rother, and boasts a two-storey curtain wall with castellated parapet, four round towers three-storeys high, complete with arrow slits, two rectangular towers, and a three-storey gatehouse equipped with a further four towers with murder holes from which boiling oil and water could be poured. However, venture inside and you will find naught but a shell.

Bodiam Castle was the brainchild of Sir Edward Dalyngrigge (c. 1346–93). With no prospect of an inheritance, he took himself off to France to make his fortune as a mercenary soldier in the One Hundred Years War (1337–1453). Plunder was the order of the day and Dalyngrigge clearly did rather well. He then made a good marriage to Elizabeth Wardeux in 1378, which brought him the Manor of Bodiam. He gradually elevated his status, acquiring a number of local offices including Justice of the Peace, Collector of Taxes and Member of Parliament.

Perhaps wary of the possibility of his new estate's proximity to the Sussex Coast, and French and Spanish raids on ports in Kent and Sussex, Dalyngrigge sought the King's permission to fortify his house against the possibility of attack. He was not alone in doing so – defences were being constructed all along the South Coast. The long war had left the exchequer short of funds and the straitened Navy was struggling to patrol and protect the English Channel properly.

The King gave permission for Dalyngrigge to: 'strengthen with a wall of stone … and construct

LEFT With its towers and wide moat, 14th-century Bodiam Castle looks almost too perfect to be true.

and make into a castle his manor house at Bodiam, near the sea in the county of Sussex, for the defence of the adjacent county and resistance to our enemies.' However, Dalyngrigge opted to build an entirely new fortified castle that visually asserted his status and power, rather than simply securing his existing home as part of coastal-defence scheme.

The effectiveness of Bodiam Castle has been much debated. Although on the surface it appears to have been constructed as a fortification, in reality there were a number of weaknesses in the design: the gun sills are angled so that hardly anything can be seen within near range; the moat could be easily drained; the castle walls are little more than screens; the watch towers on the turrets simply top the stairwells; and four huge windows are a point of weakness. In his essay 'Kings and Castles: court life in peace and war' the medieval scholar Christopher Hohler described Bodiam as: 'an old soldier's dream-house' and maintained it could never have played a significant part in a late 14th-century war.

Though little of the interior remains, it is apparent that the castle once contained a chapel, a service hall and kitchen, private chambers, an impressive 33 fireplaces and 28 garderooms – storage rooms or toilets – as well as stables and a dovecote, which perhaps indicates that Dalyngrigge had intended to station a garrison within the castle, but as he died around the time of its completion he never had the chance to see his plans become a reality.

When the Dalyngrigge male line died out in 1470, the castle passed into the hands of the Lewknor family through marriage. Sir Thomas Lewknor provoked the wrath of Yorkist King Richard III through his support of the House of Lancaster, and Bodiam Castle was besieged by royal forces in 1484 and surrendered to the Crown, though it was later restored to Sir Thomas by Henry VII after his victory at Bosworth Field (1485).

Uninhabited from the 16th century, Bodiam was sold by the Lewknor family to Nicholas Tufton in 1623; thereafter it changed hands many more times, on some occasions for the express purpose of asset stripping. Bodiam remained in a ruinous state, but its scenic charm attracted the attention of artists such as J. M. W. Turner, whose works have subsequently been scrutinised for clues to the castle's lost structures.

Threats of demolition were averted in 1829 by John 'Mad Jack' Fuller, a retired politician. Noted for his fondness for alcohol, gambling and follies, and notorious for his defence of slavery, Fuller purchased Bodiam Castle at auction for £3,000, a purchase that highlights the early beginnings of the building conservation movement. After Fuller's death, the castle was sold to George Cubitt Lord Ashdown, in 1864, who undertook some restoration work. This was enthusiastically continued by its final owner, Lord Curzon, former Viceroy of India who purchased Bodiam in 1916. Curzon bequeathed the Castle to the National Trust in 1926.

MAUNSELL FORTS, THAMES ESTUARY

In 1939 the Port of London was one of the busiest ports in the world and, with the outbreak of war, Germany sought to prevent essential supplies from America and the Empire reaching Britain via this route. Targeting the Thames Estuary, the Germans utilised a new weapon, the magnetic mine, that was to prove disastrous for the British war effort. These mines detonated only when in the proximity of a large magnetic object such as a ship. In the first few months of the war over 100 vessels were sunk, effectively closing shipping routes while the mines were cleared. Prime Minister Winston Churchill ordered the construction of forts in the open sea to break up enemy aircraft formations approaching the port, Guy Maunsell (1884–1961) an engineer and former soldier, was charged with their design.

Dubbed Maunsell Forts, these nautical bastions are regarded as the predecessors of modern offshore rigs. They stood on a reinforced-concrete pontoon base, with twin supporting towers – essentially bunkers – creating seven floors of accommodation sturdy enough to withstand explosions. The towers were linked above the waterline by a steel platform deck that could support other structures, and placements for anti-aircraft guns, radar installations and searchlights. The forts, said to weigh some 4,500 tonnes, were constructed in dry dock, then towed into position and winched onto sandbanks off the coasts of Kent and Essex; they were also used in the Mersey Estuary to protect the docks at Liverpool.

The first forts were manned by the navy and accommodated 120 men and three officers. Like lighthouse keepers, the men were on duty for six weeks at a time. In 1943 three larger forts designed by Maunsell were installed to provide further protection for London. Named Shivering Sands, Red Sands and Nore Army Fort, they were more futuristic in design with a central control tower linked to six satellites. These were manned by the army and accommodated 265 men.

The forts surprised German air crews, who did not expect to come under fire flying over water. Between them, the forts shot down 22 planes and destroyed around 30 flying bombs. Maunsell went on to design the Mulberry Harbours used for the D-Day landings in Normandy in 1944.

Maintenance crews were kept in place on the forts until 1956, but all were decommissioned by the late 1950s. The Liverpool forts were demolished in the 1950s as they were a danger to shipping. There was a less focused approach with those in the Thames; some were destroyed following collisions with civilian ships, and some by the weather.

In the mid-1960s Shivering Sands was home to pirate-radio operators. Screaming Lord Sutch, musician and founder of the Monster Raving Loony Party, broadcast in the summer of 1964, then sold the operation to his manager, Reginald Calvert, who created the station Radio City. Calvert was later shot dead in a pirate radio broadcasting fracas. The Marine Broadcasting Offences Act was passed in 1967 outlawing all such activity and the pirate-radio operators moved out.

Fort Roughs is the site of the self-proclaimed Principality of Sealand; it was founded in 1967 by Roy and Joan Bates and claims to be the world's smallest nation, complete with flag.

Red Sands fort is the only fort surviving more or less intact; it lost one leg in a shipping collision. A group of enthusiasts hope to restore it to its original condition.

LEFT The Red Sands Sea Forts lie near the mouth of the River Thames.

RACTON MONUMENT, WEST SUSSEX

The famously extravagant 18th-century statesman George Montagu-Dunk, the 2nd Earl of Halifax (1716–71), had a fondness for follies and cricket. He was bequeathed Stansted Park near the Hampshire–Sussex border in 1766 by an uncle, and set about constructing Racton Monument, sometimes dubbed Racton Tower.

Quite where he found the time is another matter. Montagu-Dunk was President of the Board of Trade between 1748 and 1761 and actively promoted colonial development. He helped found the capital of Nova Scotia in Canada which was promptly named Halifax in his honour. Indeed, there are an assortment of Halifax towns, a river and a county in the United States all called Halifax after him, as are the Australian islands of Dunk and Montague.

The 2nd Earl of Halifax went on to be Lord Lieutenant of Ireland between 1761 and 1763, was briefly First Lord of the Admiralty in 1762, and was appointed Secretary of State in the same year. He was made Lord Privy Seal in 1770, and returned to the post of Secretary of State in 1770, a position he retained until his death in June 1771.

This range of appointments should have been enough to keep him out of mischief, but on acquiring Stansted Park in his fiftieth year, Montagu-Dunk promptly commissioned the young architect Theodosius Keene to design two follies. One was an Ionic temple that was destroyed by fire during the Second World War, the other, Racton Tower, lay outside the estate around 400m (¼ mile) from the house. This four-storey building, constructed in red brick and faced in flint, was triangular in shape with a round turret on each corner and reached over 24m (80ft) in height. Montagu-Dunk may well have died before his towering folly was ever completed. He left no children, and his titles died with him.

As a folly, Racton Monument has no apparent purpose, though when it was built it would have commanded fine views over the sea. Today this graffitied tower is in private ownership. Over the years it has been the scene of several suicides and is reputed to have been the site of occult practices.

RIGHT AND BELOW The magnificent flint-faced folly that is Racton Mounment.

PORTCHESTER CASTLE, HAMPSHIRE

In the 3rd century AD the Romans constructed a series of nine Saxon Shore forts along the south coast to protect themselves against Saxon raids from Germany. *Portus Adurni* was designed to function as a supply base for *Classis Britannica*, the provincial fleet of the Roman navy whose job it was to control the English Channel (*Mare Britannicum*) and the water around the Roman Province of Britannia.

The fort was encircled by a massive 6m (20ft) stone curtain wall, intersected with 20 bastions (circular and semi-circular towers). This stout construction was designed to withstand siege, for the Romans had learned that it was not always advantageous to attack.

Archaeological evidence indicates that occupation continued in some form after the Romans withdrew from Britain in the 5th century. By 904 *Portus Adurni* was a prosperous fortified town – or burh – that could be defended against Viking raids.

After the Norman Conquest in 1066, William I granted the manor of Portchester to his supporter William Mauduit, who began construction of the castle, utilising stone from the Roman fort. The keep was expanded, and more floors added in the 12th century. The site is so large that an Augustinian priory was founded here in 1128. The monks departed after just 22 years, but their church became the parish church for Portchester village.

In 1153 Henry Maudit, a descendant of the founder, was granted the castle by Henry of Anjou, but when he ascended the throne as Henry II a year later, he rather churlishly took it back. The castle remained in royal ownership until 1632. Edward III (1327–77) stayed before crossing to France for the Battle of Crécy in 1346, and in 1415 Henry V (c.1387–1422) launched his invasion of France from Portchester, culminating in his victory at Agincourt.

But the castle was also a royal pleasure palace; King John (1166–1216) was a regular visitor and he enjoyed hunting in the nearby Forest of Bere. Richard II (1377–c.1399) built a series of luxurious royal apartments. Henry VI's French bride Margaret of Anjou landed here in 1445, and Elizabeth I held court here in 1603.

The Royal Dockyard at Portsmouth was founded in 1495, and as the town grew, Portchester Castle fell from royal favour. In 1632 Charles I (1600–49) sold it to Sir William Uvedale. During the Civil War (1642–51) Parliamentary troops were garrisoned here. Soon after, in the Anglo-Dutch wars, 500 Dutch prisoners were held at Portchester Castle. Much later, during the Napoleonic Wars (1793–1815) up to 8,000 prisoners were confined here; 2,000 of their number were former French slaves from St Lucia. Prisoners were released when hostilities ended in 1814 and the prison was closed in 1819.

Both the Saxon Shore fort and Portchester Castle have been in the care of English Heritage since 1984.

RIGHT Portchester Castle is encircled by the fortified walls of a Roman Fort.

NYMANS,
WEST SUSSEX

During the night of 20 February 1947, a fire started in the magnificent country house of Lt Col. Leonard Messel and his wife Maud. Leonard raised the alarm and 70 firefighters struggled to gain control of the blaze in the village of Handcross, West Sussex, but in the bitterly cold weather all the nearby sources of water were frozen, making their task nigh on impossible. The loss of the majority of the house and its contents, which included three Gainsboroughs, a Velázquez and a Rembrandt, was reported in the national newspapers.

The arresting ruins of this 'medieval' manor house still stand in the midst of the magnificent garden at Nymans, but in actuality, the house was comparatively new – a glorious piece of pseudo-medieval artifice completed just 19 years earlier.

Ludwig Messel (1847–1915), a Jewish émigré from a banking family in the region of Hessen-Darmstadt in Germany, arrived in England in 1868; it is said that he had gold coins sewn into his shirt to finance his new life. Ludwig worked as a clerk in an American stockbroking firm, and within five years of his arrival had set up the stockbroking house of L. Messel & Co. in the City of London. In quick succession he married, became a

LEFT Nymans was devastated by a terrible fire just over 30 years after it was completed.

British subject, and in 1890 purchased Nymans as a country residence – the expansion of the railways was turning Sussex into a new commuter belt.

When not working in London, Ludwig Messel devoted 25 years to creating a magnificent garden in his 243ha (600 acres), working with garden designers William Robinson and Gertrude Jekyll, the latter influencing the garden's informal planting schemes.

On Ludwig Messel's death his son Leonard received a large inheritance that included Nymans. He and his wife Maud moved there with some misgivings, describing it as a 'nondescript Regency house'. However, the garden tempted them and so it was decided they should dispense with much of the old house and create their dream home. Sir Walter Tapper and the interestingly named Norman Evill were employed to redesign the house in a late Gothic-Tudor style to complement Leonard and Maud's preferred style of interior decor. Maud's daughter Anne, (mother of Antony Armstrong-Jones, later Lord Snowdon) used to say that her mother fantasised about living in a medieval manor house in the West Country.

The design of Nymans was highly praised, and, together with the garden, it frequently featured in magazines such as *Country Life*. The family enjoyed

company and played host to the aristocracy, academics and artists alike and threw fabulous fancy-dress parties. Their younger son, Oliver Messel, went on to become a painter and a set and costume designer for both theatre and film.

The 1947 fire destroyed most of the house and its contents, including Leonard's acclaimed collection of gardening books and herbals. Even though one wing of the house was made habitable, the Messels were devastated.

Leonard bequeathed the estate to the National Trust on his death in 1953 in order that the garden be maintained. Initially the Trust did not pay too much attention to the picturesque ruins of the house, but as they decayed the decision was made to preserve the ruins as a worthy reflection of 20th-century romanticism.

The Messel's daughter Anne, Countess of Rosse, returned to live in the renovated wing after the death of her second husband in 1979. She sought to restore the décor and atmosphere of the original house and remained at Nymans until her death in 1992. She was the last member of the family to reside there.

LEFT AND FAR LEFT Sir Walter Tapper and Norman Evill designed Nymans in a late Gothic Tudor style.

South East and East 61

ORFORD NESS, SUFFOLK

Lying on the Suffolk coast is the remote shingle spit of Orford Ness, said to be the largest vegetated spit in Europe, a rare and fragile habitat with a wealth of wildlife. It is a Site of Special Scientific Interest, a National Nature Reserve, and an internationally important Natura 2000 and Ramsar-designated wetland site. For long periods of the 20th century this isolated spot has also served as a vast military research centre, the work at which was instrumental in influencing the outcomes of both World Wars and the Cold War.

Orford was a prosperous port until deposits from the North Sea created a burgeoning shingle spit, altering the coastal geography, and by the late Middle Ages sea trade was significantly reduced. This Ness – or nose – had marshlands, reedbeds, tidal creeks, lagoons and a vast expanse of shingle. It was the isolation of this spot that attracted the attention of the War Office in 1913, which was on the hunt for just such a location to be used for top-secret military experimentation. The government promptly purchased the site which it utilised through two World Wars and during the Cold War.

Public access was immediately restricted, and sea defences improved. A flying field, with air strips, was established on King's Marshes, and this was serviced by aircraft hangers and a light-gauge railway, as well

as workshops and accommodation for over 600 personnel. Materials for all this construction were shipped from Orford Quay.

Here, away from prying eyes, aircraft, guns and bomb sights were tested and evaluated. Night-navigation systems were practised, and research undertaken to resolve the technical difficulties encountered in flying in action.

From 1924 more buildings and a new range were constructed to test ballistics by checking the flight behaviours and effects of bombs and other projectiles. In 1935 a small team, led by Robert Watson-Watt, conducted top-secret experiments in radio direction finding – later called radar technology – with the purpose of developing an air defence system. The historian A. J. P. Taylor stated that the systems they developed were fundamental to Britain's victory in the Second World War.

In 1953 the Atomic Weapons Research Establishment took over the site to undertake pioneering work testing the development of nuclear weapons. This required the construction of a new roads and bridges, together with buildings that served as headquarters, control rooms and laboratories. Two huge reinforced concrete laboratories, later dubbed the pagodas, were constructed in 1960–62; the concrete walls were 3m (10ft) thick and the roofs weighed some 1,500 tonnes. These labs were designed for environmental testing, such as vibration, and

RIGHT The original electrical fittings remain at Orford Ness.

FAR RIGHT The concrete pagodas with their distinctive roofs designed to contain explosive blasts.

FOLLOWING PAGE The Bomb Ballistics building seen through Bailey Bridge, which crosses Stony Ditch.

theoretically to withstand a massive explosive resulting from accidental detonation, though fortuitously this feature was never put to the test. In addition, there was a thermal chamber, two centrifuges, a hard-impact target facility and a munitions store.

The last facility to be built was Cobra Mist in 1968. A vast, experimental OTH radar system with towering antennae, it was designed to monitor, amongst other things, Soviet missile and rocket launches. Some 750,000 tonnes of material were shipped to the site for its construction, which was largely funded by the United States – as economic cutbacks were inhibiting the government's capacity to develop the facility – but within six years its function was redundant, the technology being superseded by spy satellites.

The last environmental tests were conducted at Orford Ness in 1971 – much of the work undertaken there is still protected by the Official Secrets Act – after which the site was abandoned by military defence. The site continued to be used after the AWRE left (for example, by an RAF bomb disposal unit and by the BBC's World Service to broadcast to Western Europe) but never to the same scale. Aside from this, the facility was closed, though scavengers – some officially sanctioned, others not – took anything that could be moved and sold.

Orford Ness was purchased by the National Trust in 1993 and the site opened to managed public access in 1995. To protect this fragile site, visitor numbers and opening times are restricted; it is open on specific days between Easter and October, with access via a short ferry ride. Hazardous military debris still litters the Ness and visitors must keep to safe, marked trails – unexploded ordnance turns up regularly. Nevertheless this eerie site still stands, a fascinating brutalist testament to past conflict.

THE GOTHIC TOWER, WIMPOLE ESTATE, CAMBRIDGESHIRE

There has been a house at Wimpole for many centuries – indeed it is listed in the Domesday Book of 1086 as a moated manor house with deer park. As is the wont of all prosperous homeowners, politician Thomas Chicheley (1614–99) decided that having been in the family for 250 years it was time to construct a more up-to-date and commodious residence. The expansive new hall was completed in 1650 and still ranks as one of the largest houses in Cambridgeshire.

Chicheley retained ownership of Wimpole for 36 years before financial problems forced its sale 13 years before his death. The estate passed through various hands until 1740 when it was purchased, reputedly for £100,000, by the brilliant and politically astute Philip Yorke (1690–1764), 1st Earl of Hardwicke from 1733, who served as Lord Chancellor from 1737–56. Yorke commissioned the architect Sanderson Miller (1716–80), a pioneer of the Gothic Rococo style, to design a ruined folly for the grounds. The design was finally agreed upon in 1750, although work did not start until 1768, after the 1st Earl's death.

When the 2nd Earl of Hardwicke inherited Wimpole from his father, he and his wife Jemima asked Lancelot 'Capability' Brown to draw up plans for landscaping the 203ha (500 acre) estate. This included the construction of Sanderson Miller's design for the folly on Johnson's Hill in the North Park. In total, the 2nd Earl paid Brown £3,400 for the work – well in excess of £5 million in today's money.

The 3rd Earl Hardwicke employed Humphry Repton who regarded the folly as one of the best of its kind and drew up plans to make parts of it habitable, turning it into a three-bedroom home for the head gamekeeper, work which was later undertaken.

The family remained in Wimpole Hall until the late 19th century when the extravagant lifestyle of the 5th Earl Charles Yorke, saw the property taken in lieu of debts by Thomas Agar-Robartes, the 6th Viscount Clifden (curiously Wimpole had been home to his ancestors in the late 17th century). The folly continued to be used as a gamekeeper's cottage until the 1920s, when it was left to fall into a genuinely ruinous state of structural collapse.

Wimpole Hall was bequeathed to the National Trust in 1976 by Elsie Bambridge, Rudyard Kipling's daughter, who had purchased it in 1938 with the help of royalties from her father's books. The Trust undertook complex restoration work to preserve the Grade II-listed folly, revealing the artifice behind the original construction of this sham ruin. The Gothic tower was made of red brick but faced with finely dressed chalk stone – clunch – to give the impression of age. This had left it vulnerable to erosion and abetted the collapse of its crenellation. After being closed to the public for 30 years Wimpole Folly is close to being fully restored to its original ruinous design and the base and grounds around the folly were opened to the public in 2015. It stands as a testament to the extravagant aesthetic ideals of the 18th-century Picturesque movement.

RIGHT This ruined Gothic folly was designed by Sanderson Miller.

MIDLANDS AND THE NORTH

MIDLANDS AND THE NORTH

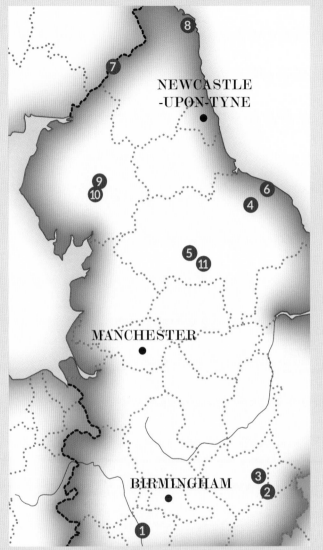

Snaking across the north of England for 118km (73 miles), Hadrian's Wall highlights the long history of tension between the Scots and their southern invaders. Skirmishes were a common occurrence south of the border but being prepared to defend the north in the name of the King was the price the landed gentry had to pay to maintain royal favour. Great castles and strategically located tower houses were constructed to defend extensive estates. Whole generations of young men were wiped out in the ongoing struggles. Meanwhile in Yorkshire, vast tracts of empty countryside were handed over to the Cistercians, who founded monasteries such as Rievaulx Abbey (see pages 80–83) and Fountains Abbey (see pages 84–89), where they could practise self-sufficiency and worship in peace. The Midlands and the North saw the construction of grand country homes. Nobles bankrupted themselves building palaces fit for a queen, a fate that befell poor Sir Christopher Hatton with Kirby Hall (see pages 76–79), in the faint hope that the royal person could be tempted by the prospect of a sleepover. Businessmen and industrialists spent lavishly on great mansions that reflected their newly elevated status, indulging in displays of extravagance that more often than not saw them, or their descendants, being carted off to debtor's prison, and their homes abandoned.

1 WITLEY COURT
2 LYVEDEN NEW BIELD
3 KIRBY HALL
4 RIEVAULX ABBEY
5 FOUNTAINS ABBEY
6 WHITBY ABBEY

7 HADRIAN'S WALL
8 DUNSTANBURGH CASTLE
9 BROUGHAM CASTLE
10 LOWTHER CASTLE
11 HAREWOOD CASTLE

PREVIOUS PAGE
Dunstanburgh Castle.

LEFT The magnificent ruin of Fountains Abbey.

WITLEY COURT, WORCESTERSHIRE

Witley Court is a prime example of a house that never quite matched up to the aspirations of its owners. Since its earliest incarnation as a Saxon manor house it has been relentlessly extended, improved and redesigned. Its ruins stand testament to the human desire for self-aggrandisement.

The early days of Whitley Court were quiet and stable, but when it came into the hands of the Russell family, who had long served as members of parliament for Wytley, they tore down the existing house and constructed a substantial red-brick Jacobean pile. It was sold by Francis Russell in 1655 to Thomas Foley (1617–77), the son of an iron merchant. Under his stewardship the family business had boomed, and Foley invested the profits in purchasing estates, and the family quietly began its transition from industry to public service. Thomas' grandson became Baron Foley of Kidderminster. He expanded the house significantly, adding new wings on each side.

In the 18th century the grounds were extensively landscaped, a lake was created at the front of the house by damming a brook and planting an ornamental woodland. Just as the family's financial fortunes were on the wane, Thomas Foley VII commissioned the leading Regency architect John Nash to extensively remodel the house, with hindsight one expansion too many for this, the Foley family seat for over 180 years.

In 1837 Thomas Foley, 4th Baron Foley, sold Witley Court to William, Lord Ward, later Earl of Dudley, to clear family debts for £890,000. Ward, who had inherited a fortune from family interests in coal and iron, lent the house to Queen Adelaide, the widow of William IV, between 1843 and 1846.

When she departed, the Earl of Dudley commissioned the architect Samuel Daukes to redesign Witley Court, and over the course of the next ten years it was transformed into a stunning neo-Palladian mansion. William Andrews Nesfield, the leading landscape designer of the day, was brought in to rethink the grounds. His grand scheme included formal parterres and, as its centrepiece, the magnificent spouting Perseus and Andromeda fountain.

As Ward's fortune diminished, the house was emptied and put up for sale in 1920 and the vast estates parcelled up and sold off in lots. The house was acquired by Sir Herbert Smith, a carpet manufacturer from Kidderminster. Despite Smith's wealth he struggled to maintain the house and it was neglected. On 7 September 1937, when the family were absent, the head housekeeper spotted that the roof above the servant's rooms was on fire. Fanned by wind, the blaze spread rapidly and despite the best efforts of the servants it could not be contained. The next day Witley Court was a smouldering ruin. One side of the house was unaffected, but as Sir Herbert had been unable to insure the house, the cost of rebuilding was prohibitive. The once great Witley Court was sold for scrap, stripped bare and abandoned.

The Department of the Environment took the house into its care in 1972, saving it from complete destruction, and it was put under the guardianship of English Heritage. Today the shell of the house stands, and the gardens and the immense Perseus and Andromeda fountain – which noisily shoots water over 30m (100ft) into the air – have been extensively restored.

LEFT The neo-Palladian mansion of Witley Court was devastated by fire in 1937.

LYVEDEN NEW BIELD, NORTHAMPTONSHIRE

Despite never having been completed, the shell of Lyveden New Bield is a protected Grade I-listed building; a stark reminder of the impact of religious turmoil in the 16th and 17th centuries.

In 1468 Thomas Tresham, who owned an estate at nearby Rushton, expanded his property portfolio with the purchase of the estate at Lyveden, which came complete with two deserted medieval villages and the ruins of a moated manor house. Lewis Tresham constructed Lyveden House in the early 17th century. This L-shaped two-storey building with fashionably large mullioned windows and a stone slate roof is commonly referred to Lyveden Old Bield. As well as building this new home, the family considerably extended its lands to reflect their elevated status.

In 1559 the estate passed to Thomas Tresham's 15-year-old great-grandson – also Thomas – who was orphaned at the age of three. A clever and bookish young man, Tresham studied law and corresponded with Queen Elizabeth I's Secretary of State, William Cecil, and her Lord Chancellor Christopher Hatton.

Tresham became Sheriff of Northamptonshire in 1573 and was knighted by the Queen two years later. Life should have been pleasant. He had money, rank and 11 children with his wife Muriel Throckmorton.

However, Tresham and his family were, in secret, devout Catholics. Initially tolerant of papists, Elizabeth I's security was threatened by Catholic plots to depose her. Over the course of her reign she gradually approved harsher penalties against Catholics who would not attend Anglican services. Just six years after Tresham was knighted he was arrested and hauled before the Privy Council for charges including harbouring a Jesuit priest, and receiving mass. Between 1581 and 1593 he was fined and spent long periods imprisoned or placed under house arrest for his continued refusal to swear the Oath of Allegiance to the queen.

On his release in 1592, Tresham drew up plans to build an elaborate garden and garden lodge house on the estate. Lyveden New Bield (also known as the Lodge) was designed in the shape of the Catholic cross and its walls painted with religious friezes and inscriptions in an emphatic and provocative statement of belief.

Tresham died on the 11th September 1605, leaving his vision incomplete and debts of £11,000 – equating to over £2 million in today's money. But the family's problems did not end there, because shortly after Tresham's death, his son Francis was arrested for his part in the Gunpowder Plot. Francis died before he could be put to trial, his cause of death unclear. Some historians cite a urinary-tract infection, others suggest he may have been poisoned.

When news of his arrest reached the men working on Lyveden New Bield they downed tools and abandoned the site. The Tresham's continued to be persecuted for their Catholic beliefs which led to them finally being relieved of Lyveden Estate in lieu of debts in the mid-17th century. The National Trust acquired Lyveden in 1922 and work is underway to incorporate Lyveden Manor, and Tresham's design, into the property.

RIGHT Tresham's vision for Lyveden New Bield was a statement of religious belief.

KIRBY HALL, NORTHAMPTONSHIRE

In 1830 the Rev. Canon James evocatively described the desolation of Kirby Hall thus: 'the very action of decomposition going on, the crumbling stucco of the ceiling feeding the vampire ivy, the tattered tapestry yet hanging on the wall, the picture flapping in its broken frame.' In just over 250 years the glory days of the house, once the height of innovative Renaissance design, had degenerated into a ruin.

Construction of the house in Rockingham Forest, Northamptonshire, was instigated by Sir Humphrey Stafford in 1570. The quasi-French design, lifted from French pattern books, spared the need for an architect. It featured elements of classical architecture and immediately stood out as a cosmopolitan building of architectural merit. However, Sir Humphrey died just as the house was nearing completion.

Kirby Hall was snapped up in 1575 by Sir Christopher Hatton (1540–91), a courtier and favourite of Queen Elizabeth I, who showered him with gifts, appointments and grants. Hatton, motivated by the same ambitions as his predecessor, immediately ordered further works at Kirby Hall, and unusually for the time made the inward-facing house outward facing, adding the vast bow windows on the front which looked out over the estate. He also had the village of Kirby-in-Gretton demolished to allow him to extend the park. Incredibly his first visit to Kirby Hall was not until 1583.

Prior even to the purchase of Kirby, Hatton had already embarked on the total reconstruction of Holdenby Hall, his family seat, determined to make it the largest private house in Elizabethan England. He attained the position of Lord Chancellor, then fell from royal favour, nudged out of position by younger favourites. The Queen heartlessly asked for repayment of the royal loans that had enabled Sir Christopher to fund his ambitious property schemes. Hatton died in 1591, unmarried and childless, with debts of £40,000, and still slavishly devoted to Elizabeth.

Hatton's initials can still be seen carved into the stone porch at Kirby, along with his family symbol, a golden hind, an emblem that was utilised on one of England's most famous ships in his honour. Sir Christopher funded the voyages of Francis Drake and in return insisted that his secretary, Mr Doughty, accompany the adventurer on his attempt to circumnavigate the globe in 1577. Relations became fraught on the voyage and Doughty challenged Drake's authority and was subsequently executed for treason. In a bid to appease his patron Drake renamed his ship *The Golden Hind*.

Kirby Hall passed to Hatton's nephew, Sir William Newport, who adopted the name of Christopher Hatton,

FAR LEFT A view through the loggia to the east range of Kirby Hall.

LEFT The iron door handle on the main porch.

and the house became the main family residence in 1608 (Holdenby Hall was sold to James I in 1607). The family continued to name their eldest sons Christopher, and a whole series of Christopher Hattons put their fashionable mark on the house.

The house was eventually honoured by a visit from royalty. Baron Hatton, Christopher Hatton III (1605–1670) had created widely admired gardens and King James I of England and his wife Anne of Denmark visited four times between 1612 and 1624, taking over the entire south-west wing for the duration of their stay. Sir Christopher was a prominent royalist and Charles I was also entertained at Kirby Hall. Inigo Jones was employed to redecorate its exterior in 1640.

In 1764 Kirby Hall passed via the female line to the Earls of Winchilsea, and the name Finch-Hatton was adopted. Unfortunately for Kirby the family home was in Kent and it was little used, as well as being incredibly costly to upkeep. In the 1800s the lead was stripped from the roof, the wainscoting from the walls, and the furniture and statuary sold. At one time the only inhabitant was the estate shepherd and his flock. The 12th Earl of Winchilsea, Murray Finch-Hatton (1851–1898), tried to save the house from complete ruin and used to say that if ever his ship came in, he would restore the house completely.

Kirby, a roofless ruin, was taken into the care of the Office of Works, a forerunner to English Heritage, in 1935. It is still owned by the Earls of Winchilsea, but is managed and maintained by English Heritage.

LEFT The view from the north side of Kirby Hall's inner court.

RIEVAULX ABBEY, NORTH YORKSHIRE

When Rievaulx Abbey came into the guardianship of His Majesty's Office of Works in 1917 it was in a state of imminent collapse. A survey found its walls shrouded with ivy, its floors strewn with rubble and buried under carpet upon carpet of soil. Since its dissolution on 3 December 1538, Rievaulx had been left to rot, a ruin for longer than it had been a working abbey. In the intervening years it had served as an ironworks, a charcoal store, a working farm and, from the 18th century, a burgeoning tourist attraction.

Work to clear the site began in 1919: an estimated 90,000 tonnes of soil were removed from the Abbey ruins, exposing the buried sections and uncovering thousands of objects, including stonework, metalwork, pottery and glass. Labour was provided by war veterans, and pioneering engineering works stabilised the buildings. That it had survived so long was a testament to its builders for the sheer scale of Rievaulx Abbey is astounding.

It sits on a 405ha (1,000 acre) site beside the River Rye, on land donated by Walter Espec, Lord of Helmsley, a supporter of ecclesiastical reform. Founded in 1132 by 12 monks from Clairvaux Abbey in France

RIGHT A detail of stone carving from Rievaulx Abbey.

FAR RIGHT The arches on the south side of the presbytery from the east end of the abbey church. Grass now carpets the presbytery and birds sing where the choir stalls would have been.

– the root of the Cistercian movement – the early buildings were constructed in timber, with stone being utilised from the late 1130s. Abbot Aelred, who arrived as a postulant in 1134, oversaw its phenomenal growth and development. By his death in 1167 the community had almost quadrupled in size with some 140 monks and 500 lay brothers – recruits from itinerant poor living and working there and undertook nearly all of the hard labour.

By now the Abbey was monumental in size and included cloisters, an infirmary hall, a refectory, a lodge for the Abbot, a warming house and kitchen, gardens, orchards and even a water-powered forge where the lay brothers smelted ore to make tools, nails and cutlery as required. Even the river was twice rerouted to suit their needs.

In the 1220s the abbey was further extended to create a shrine for Abbot Aelred, but budgetary constraints meant the work was only partially completed. By the 14th century things were looking considerably less rosy; the area was plundered by the Scots after the 1322 Battle of Old Byland in the Wars of Scottish Independence, and the Black Death wreaked havoc in the area. Finding their prospects less attractive, the lay brothers departed. By the time the monastery was

dissolved, there were just 23 monks in the community together with 102 'servants and attendants'.

The land was sold to Thomas Manners, 1st Earl of Rutland, who partially dismantled the buildings and developed the existing ironworks. The ironworks were kept in service until the middle of the 17th century. The Rye Valley, including the ruins of Rievaulx, was sold in 1687 to Sir Charles Duncombe, an immensely wealthy banker. The family constructed Duncombe Park on their land and further extended their estate. Thomas Duncombe created a terrace above Rievaulx, complete with classical temples, to provide the ultimate romantic view. This act partially secured Rievaulx's future because as the fame of this picturesque view grew the visitors began to arrive.

Nevertheless, the Duncombe family refused to allow any excavation of the site and were unwilling to pay for repairs, though they did restore the Abbey's slipper chapel so that it could serve as the parish church. With the passing of the Ancient Monument Protection Act in 1882 the owners of historic sites were encouraged to hand them over to the guardianship of the state. In 1913 the Ancient Monuments Consolidation and Amendment Act gave the Office of Works the power to place protective measures around any monument they deemed worthy of protection – with or without the owner's consent.

Rievaulx Abbey was to become one of the Office of Works' earliest acquisitions. Negotiations stalled with the outbreak of The First World War, but after Charles Duncombe, 2nd Earl of Feversham was killed at the Battle of Flers–Courcelette during the Somme offensive, Rievaulx came into the guardianship of the Ministry, now English Heritage, and its future was secured. The Terrace has been in the care of the National Trust since 1976.

LEFT Thomas Duncombe created a terrace above Rievaulx Abbey to create a picturesque view.

FOUNTAINS ABBEY, NORTH YORKSHIRE

Fountains Abbey, Britain's largest monastic ruin, was founded in 1132 by a group of Benedictine monks. They had broken away from St Mary's Benedictine Abbey in York wanting to join a reformed monastic order. The Archbishop of York provided the monks, who he described as 'learned men all seeking the true observance of their rule', with a parcel of land in the valley of the River Skell in North Yorkshire.

The site was described in chronicles as an 'inhospitable valley thickset with thorns … Fit rather to the lair of wild beasts than the home of human beings.' After a harsh winter in 1133 – the monks were said to be in a continual state of near starvation and two of their number returned to the comparative luxury of St Mary's Abbey – they applied to join the Cistercian Order and in 1135 were accepted. A monk was despatched from Clairvaux in France to educate the monks in the ways of the Order, and to show them how to construct buildings in accordance with Cistercian practice: plain, unadorned and elegantly severe. Unfortunately, their situation remained desperate and the Abbot begged leave to abandon Fountains and join the mother house in France. The future of the Abbey looked bleak, but it was saved by the timely arrival of two new recruits bearing money and books.

Unlike other Cistercian monasteries, which seemed to prosper steadily until the 14th century, Fountains' fortunes fluctuated wildly. In 1146 the Abbey was attacked by an angry mob protesting against the Abbot's opposition to their favoured candidate for Archbishop of York. Fountains Abbey also suffered boom or bust according to who was in charge. Many abbots struggled with the varied demands of this often unsought position; managing the Abbey's separate parcels of land endowments, which brought in income, was an administrative nightmare. Moreover, the job of abbot was not without its risks; Abbot William Thirsk of Fountains Abbey, and his neighbour Abbot Adam de Sedbergh of Jervaulx Abbey, were executed by Henry VIII for supposedly plotting together against him.

Like its neighbour Rievaulx Abbey, Fountains suffered economic reverses in the 14th century with poor harvests, raids from the Scots and the Black Death (1348–50), all having an impact. However, their lot had improved by 1535; with an annual income of £1,173 not only was Fountains Abbey the wealthiest Cistercian house in Yorkshire, it was also the second wealthiest in the country, and eventually – inevitably – became a target for Henry VIII's programme of dissolution.

The Abbey was surrendered to the King in November 1539, and was sold in 1540 to Richard Gresham, who was still happily stripping lead from the roof four years later. In 1597 it passed to Stephen Proctor, who used

LEFT A stone angel, originally carved and fitted to cover a crack in one of the arched windows. The scroll carries the date 1883 – perhaps the date at which the statue was fitted to prevent further cracking.

FAR LEFT Food was once stored in the vaulted cellarium at Fountains Abbey.

FOLLOWING PAGE A view from the east site hints at the expansive scale of Fountains Abbey.

stone from the ruins to build Fountains Hall in 1604. Fountains Abbey then changed hands several times before being purchased in 1767 for £18,000 by one William Aislabie from the neighbouring estate of Studley Royal.

Aislabie's father, John, a former Chancellor of the Exchequer, had been expelled from Parliament and disqualified from public office for life for his promotion of the South Sea Company, which had collapsed spectacularly in 1720. After a spell in the gatehouse of the Tower of London, the disgraced MP returned to Yorkshire and devoted his remaining years to developing his garden. After his father's death, William followed his lead, and with the purchase of the Severn Bridges Valley and Fountains Abbey, he was able to be even more ambitious; the ruins were to become one of the garden's central features and thus the Aislabies had an active interest in its preservation.

In 1843 one A. E. Hargrove described a visit to the Abbey: 'This delightful place is open to the public every day, Sundays excepted … the grounds are entirely enclosed and cannot be seen without the attendance of a guide, who will always be found at readiness … the customary fee is half-a-crown.' With the coming of the railway to Ripon just five years later the number of tourists visiting the area soared and Fountains and Studley, now forever linked, prospered. With the ruins of Fountains Abbey at its heart, this site is now recognised as one of the finest scenic compositions in England, and in 1986 it was listed by the world heritage organisation UNESCO.

The great house at Studley Royal was destroyed by fire in 1946, and the last private owners sold the Abbey ruins and garden to West Riding and North Yorkshire county councils in 1966. The National Trust took over the site in 1983.

LEFT AND RIGHT
Fountains Abbey was an ongoing building project for 400 years, and has been a ruin for a similar time.

WHITBY ABBEY, NORTH YORKSHIRE

On 16 December 1914, the German navy conducted a raid on Scarborough, Hartlepool and Whitby, laying mines and conducting an aerial bombardment. Two German warships came within 1.6km (1 mile) of Whitby and in a 15-minute attack some 200 shells were fired at the town; one missed its target, the coastguard station, and hit the west front of Whitby Abbey causing some damage. Ironically this was nothing compared to the damage caused by over 400 years of neglect.

Whitby Abbey was founded in AD657 by Oswiu, the Saxon King of Northumbria (612–670). Then called Streoneshalh, it was constructed on a dramatic headland overlooking the North Sea, above the River Esk and the fishing port of Whitby. The founding abbess was St Hild of Whitby (614–680); born a Saxon princess, she abandoned secular life at the age of 33.

The building was raided repeatedly by Vikings between 867 and 870, after which the site was abandoned for 200 years. Nothing remains from this time, though excavations have revealed the layout of this original church; most of the lay buildings had been lost to the impact of coastal erosion. Nevertheless, the ruins that existed were sufficiently impressive to inspire Reinfrid, a knight in the service of William de Percy, to enter religious life and to found a new Benedictine abbey here around 1078.

The initial buildings were constructed in timber, but by 1100 a large Romanesque church had been built from stone. Between 1225 and 1250 the monastery church was rebuilt in Gothic style. Funds limited the extent of the work but rebuilding recommenced after a fundraising campaign in 1338 and continued into the late 14th century. Craftsmen created a wealth of decoration with a profusion of carved detail and moulding. On 14 December 1539 Abbot Davell surrendered Whitby Abbey to the King Henry VIII's Commissioners for Dissolution. Records indicate that there were just 22 members left in the community but it had an annual income of £437.

As was Henry VIII's wont, the Abbey land was rented to Richard Cholmley (1516–83), who took a 21-year lease on the Abbey and the core of its estates. The family turned part of the Abbot's lodgings into a family home, Cholmley House, and in the 17th century they used stone from the Abbey to help build a new north range. The lead was stripped from the roof and the building left exposed to the full force of the elements.

After initially supporting the Parliamentarians, Sir Hugh Cholmley (1600–57) performed a volte-face, siding with King Charles I during the Civil War (1642–51). He refused to surrender Scarborough Castle to Cromwell in the Great Siege of 1645 when the Royalist cause was lost. This led to the town being subject to needless bombardment, for which the townsfolk never forgave him. By way of retaliation Parliamentary forces captured and looted Cholmley House. Sir George Strickland (1782–1874) succeeded to the Cholmley estates in 1865 and in 1880 his son Charles renovated parts of the house so that it could serve as a holiday home. Since the Cholmley's acquisition, half of the Abbey had been allowed to fall and it had been plundered for stone by locals. Graves, complete with their ghoulish contents, were falling off the eroding cliffs.

The ruins of Whitby Abbey had been attracting tourists from the early 19th century, but the publication

in 1897 of Bram Stoker's *Dracula* attracted fresh interest. Stoker had stayed at a guesthouse in Whitby in July 1890. He climbed the 199 steps from the town to the Abbey, where he noted down inscriptions and names on graves, selecting from one the name Swale for Dracula's first victim. He found a book in Whitby library which mentioned the 15th-century Wallachian Prince Vlad Tepes, who impaled his enemies on wooden stakes, and heard of a shipwreck on Tate Hill Sands, off Whitby's East Cliff. These details and the drama of the Abbey combined to provide essential elements of the plot.

In March 1920 it was announced that the Strickland family were putting Whitby Abbey under the care of the Commission of Works and Public Buildings for preservation. The rubble heaped up around the walls was removed and excavation work undertaken to learn more about the site. In 1984 the Abbey passed to English Heritage where the ruins, now forever linked with Dracula's dark aesthetic, remain a place of pilgrimage for goths.

RIGHT Bram Stoker took the name of Dracula's first victim from a gravestone at Whitby Abbey.

HADRIAN'S WALL, NORTHUMBERLAND

Hadrian's Wall runs for 118km (73 miles) across Northern England, from the banks of the River Tyne on the east coast, to Solway Firth on the west coast and is the world's largest Roman artefact. The Roman Emperor Hadrian (AD76–138) instigated its construction on the northernmost limits of the Roman Province of Britannia in AD122 after his visit to Britain.

The reason for its construction has been the subject of much debate. If it was built to keep out the barbarians from the North, as was originally thought, why was it deemed necessary to construct gates at regular intervals along its length? Contemporary thinking suggests that the wall served as a means of controlling cross-border trade and migration, as well as a way of keeping a firm eye on the marauding neighbours. More than anything else, it stood as a daunting symbol of the power and might of the Roman Empire.

The wall took six years to construct, and contrary to popular belief it does not follow the Scottish border, though at points it gets close. The whole area was surveyed to determine a line that would utilise every topographical feature to best military advantage. The Whin Sill, a natural defensive ridge of dolerite that runs across stretches of Northumberland, bears the weight of Hadrian's Wall for much of its sturdy length. Most of the wall was built in stone, to a height of 4.6m (15ft), but the last 48.3km (30 miles) on the west was initially constructed from turf. There is evidence at Sycamore Gap to suggest that the wall was also rendered in lime mortar and whitewashed. At Willowford, Chesters and

Carlisle, bridges were raised over rivers to police the waterway crossings. Small gated forts, complete with barracks, were erected at 1.6km (1 mile) intervals. These were intersected with simple turrets that served as basic lookout posts.

The wall was manned more or less continually for 300 years throughout the occupation of Roman Britain. The most recent Roman coins found on the wall date from AD403–406 indicating that the Roman departure took place sometime after this date. Once abandoned, the wall was 'slighted' by the locals, and over the centuries it was pillaged for material that could be recycled in the construction of houses, castles and churches. Great chunks of its stone were utilised in the construction of the road between Carlisle and Newcastle.

Hadrian's Wall was saved by from total destruction by the efforts of a small group of enthusiasts in the 18th and 19th centuries. In 1801, the 78-year-old William Hutton (1723–1815) walked its length and detailed his findings in his book *The History of the Roman Wall*. The clergyman and antiquarian John Hodgson (1779–1845) established that the Roman Wall had been constructed on the orders of the Emperor Hadrian and not Emperor Severus, as had previously been thought. In studying artefacts, Hodgson simply took note of an inscribed stone, first found at Hotbank in 1700 but somehow overlooked. Its inscription confirmed that the wall was built at Hadrian's command.

John Clayton (1792–1890), a lawyer and antiquarian, grew up in Chesters with the Roman fort Cilurnum in

his front garden. By the time of his death he had acquired 32.2km (20 miles) of the wall, containing five forts, by purchasing small parcels of relevant land whenever they came up for sale. Clayton sought to protect his stretches of the wall by preventing the wilful removal of stone and by organising repairs. In addition, he undertook excavations, cataloguing his many finds. In 1848 he uncovered the gate at Cawfields Milecastle, indicating that the wall was not simply a defensive structure. In 1851 *The Roman Wall*, by Rev. John Collingwood Bruce (1805–92), was published. This detailed the plight of this remarkable Roman construct and brought the findings of John Clayton and John Hodgson to public attention.

Hadrian's Wall is a protected ancient monument under the 1979 Ancient Monuments and Archaeological Areas Act and it is UNESCO-listed. Stretches of the wall are protected by the National Trust, but parts are still in private ownership.

RIGHT Hadrian's wall snakes for 118km (73 miles) across Northern England. The long-distance footpath beside it runs for 135km (84 miles).

DUNSTANBURGH CASTLE, NORTHUMBERLAND

Squatting on a Northumberland promontory, atop the towering cliffs of Gull Crag, is mighty Dunstanburgh Castle. This lonely, windswept location was not the most obvious place to build a new defensive castle, but the man funding the construction, Thomas, Earl of Leicester and Lancaster (1278–1322), was not looking to construct a Borders stronghold, but rather to create a secure bolthole.

Rich and powerful, Thomas' personal wealth was second only to that of his cousin, King Edward II, he was the natural person to lead any opposition. Thomas had been a great supporter of the King's father, Edward I, and had spent ten years fighting the Scots on his behalf. On Edward II's accession in 1307, Thomas dutifully transferred allegiance to his cousin and stood by him, even when the English aristocracy began to murmur against the King's favourite, Piers Gaveston. Fatefully the cousins quarrelled, and from that moment Thomas sided with Edward II's enemies.

Gaveston was said to be handsome and athletic. He and Edward had become attached as young men, and Gaveston's fortunes rose with that of his prince. When Edward II sailed to France to marry Isabella of France, Gaveston was named regent in his absence. The nobles were enraged that the King was giving privileges to, and taking counsel from, such a non-entity. The nature of their relationship has been the subject of much debate and Edward was certainly inordinately fond of Gaveston.

In June 1312 Gaveston was kidnapped by the Earl of Warwick, a mock trial was held in Thomas' presence, and Gaveston was found guilty of treason. The next day he was taken to Blacklow Hill on one of the Earl's estates – deliberately advertising his complicity – and run through with a sword before being beheaded. It was after this that the Earl of Lancaster decided it might be timely to construct a sturdy retreat and work on Dunstanburgh Castle was underway by May 1313.

Thomas did not hold much land in Northumberland, and the small estate of Embleton, on which the castle was constructed, was not a power base for him. The King, in what may have been a conciliatory act, granted Thomas the right to crenellate at Dunstanburgh in August 1316, though in fact the work may already have been done without his permission. The design, with the cliffs on two sides and a perfect view across the land, allowed space for a farm within its enclosed walls. South of the castle, almost hidden from view, was a small but useful harbour.

There were rumours that Thomas was in league with Robert the Bruce, and certainly Dunstanburgh, just over 40.2km (25 miles) from the Scottish border, was not subject to the repeated raids by the Scots that were made on other castles in the area. Moreover, when the King went to battle the Scots in June 1314, Lancaster failed to turn up in person to support him and to add insult to injury, sent only the minimum number of troops that feudal law required. The king was heavily defeated.

The tide finally turned against the Earl of Lancaster in 1322. He was captured after the Battle of Boroughbridge and caught retreating to Dunstanburgh, which was virtually completed. He was tried for taking arms against the King and colluding with the Scots, and

RIGHT
Dunstanburgh Castle holds an imposing position on the Northumberland coast.

like Gaveston, was executed without being allowed to speak in his own defence.

Dunstanburgh was sized by the King who utilised it as Border defence for four years, before returning it to the Lancaster estate. In 1366 it came into the possession of John of Gaunt, courtesy of his wife Blanche of Lancaster. Gaunt was appointed King Richard II's Lieutenant in the North in 1380 and ordered repairs, reinforcements and modernisation at Dunstanburgh. Gaunt died in 1399 and his son, Henry Bolingbroke, defeated Richard II and took the throne as Henry IV, thus making Dunstanburgh Crown property.

The castle saw serious military action during the Wars of the Roses; it was principally held, with occasional interruption, by the Lancastrians, but ceded to the Yorkists in 1464. From this time on it fell into gradual disrepair, and by the 16th century its stone was being systematically removed. By the reign of Elizabeth I, Dunstanburgh was described as being 'in wonderful great decaye' and was virtually uninhabitable. In 1604 it was sold to the Grey family who retained the ruins until 1869, when the castle was sold, eventually passing into the care of the state in 1929.

After Norway fell into German hands in 1940, the British government needed to defend the long, isolated and vulnerable Northumberland coast from amphibious attack. The castle served as an observation post. A pillbox and gun emplacements were installed, an anti-tank ditch was dug, and the area was mined. The National Trust now manages the land on this stretch of coast, and English Heritage manages the castle.

RIGHT
Dunstanburgh Castle was constructed as a hideaway for Thomas, Earl of Leicester and Lancaster.

BROUGHAM CASTLE, CUMBRIA

Lying beside the River Eamont in Cumbria, and close to its meeting point with the River Lowther is a site of strategic importance that guards the vital route south through the Pennines to York.

The Anglo-Norman Robert de Vieuxpont was granted Westmorland by King John in 1203, and charged with controlling communications with Scotland, and securing the land. De Vieuxpont built a three-storey keep, with stone plundered from the remains of a Roman fort, and ringed it with a timber palisade. After his death, his second son (also Robert) died from wounds received at the Battle of Lewes in 1264 fighting against King Henry III, and their estate was seized by the crown.

Roger de Clifford (c.1221–86), whose Herefordshire-based family had long fought for the Crown in the Welsh Marches, negotiated the return of the de Vieuxpont's land and promptly married one of de Vieuxpont's daughters – his only successors – to secure ownership. Thereafter Brougham Castle remained with the de Clifford family and was substantially upgraded with the addition of curtain walls and a gatehouse. In acquiring this estate, the Clifford family was required to support the Crown in its military endeavours, for which it paid a terrible price, with the head of the family repeatedly being slaughtered in battle or on crusade.

De Clifford's son, Robert (1274–1314), was appointed 1st Warden of the Marches and charged with defending the border against Scotland. He was killed in the fateful Battle of Bannockburn (1314), fighting against Robert the Bruce in a rout that saw the virtual annihilation of the English army. His son Roger, 2nd Baron de Clifford, was involved in the rebellion against the King's favourite Hugh Despenser and was hanged in

1322. His brother Robert de Clifford saw Brougham attacked by the Scots in 1388 and so badly damaged that it was not listed as a fortified castle for another 30 years.

During the Wars of the Roses (1455–87), Thomas Clifford was killed in the first Battle of St Albans (1455) fighting for Henry VI, and his son John Clifford was killed six years later at the Battle of Dintingdale. The family's lands were confiscated by the victorious King Edward IV but restored after the Tudor victory at the Battle of Bosworth (1485).

After this period of turbulence, the Clifford's fortunes flourished in the 16th century and Brougham Castle even hosted a two-day visit by King James I in 1617. The de Clifford's advancement had resulted in prolonged periods of absence and the castle's subsequent neglect. All this was to change when Lady Anne Clifford, 14th Baroness de Clifford (1590–1676), took control of her considerable inheritance in 1649. She lavished care and attention on all her castles, Pendragon, Skipton, Brough and Brougham, rotating her visits to keep a close eye on her properties. Anne died at Brougham, in the same room in which her father had been born, her mother had died and where James I had slept.

The ownership of the estate passed to the Earls of Thanet via the marriage of Anne's daughter Lady Margaret Sackville. In 1714 it was decided that it was no longer necessary to maintain Brougham, which was stripped of anything of value, including the roof, and abandoned. By the 1840s the ruins were in a perilous condition and some repairs were undertaken to preserve them. In the 1920s Brougham Castle was put under the care of the Ministry of Works and is now looked after by English Heritage.

RIGHT The Clifford family paid a terrible price supporting the Crown in its ongoing fight to defend the English border with Scotland.

LOWTHER CASTLE, CUMBRIA

At first glance, Lowther Castle looks like some vast medieval pile with its pinnacles, towers and battlements. In fact, it is a piece of pseudo-Gothic artifice, constructed over seven years between 1807 and 1814. It was designed for William Lowther, 1st Earl of Lonsdale (1757–1844), by the architect Robert Smirke, who went on to design the British Museum and the Royal Opera House. Lowther Castle cost £70,000 to build and had a room for each day of the year. Now a roofless shell, the house highlights the problem of sustaining the costly management of huge old houses.

The Lowther family can trace its roots back almost 1,000 years, and has had a home beside the River Lowther in Cumbria since the 14th century. The family residences included a medieval pele tower (a tall but simple enclosing refuge and look-out), which was torn down in 1691. This was replaced with a grand Jacobean residence that was destroyed by fire in 1718.

The Lowther dynasty included flamboyant characters; Sir James Lowther (1736–1802), Earl of Lonsdale of the first creation, reputedly took as a mistress the daughter of one of his tenants. He loved her so much that when she died he could not bear to have her buried and left her lying in bed until putrefaction finally forced him to have her placed her in a glass coffin. This he kept in a cupboard for a time before she was eventually laid to rest in Paddington cemetery. What his wife thought of this has not been recorded.

The 5th Earl, Hugh Lowther (1857–1944), was famously profligate, maintaining a private orchestra and a fleet of yellow cars; his fondness for the colour led to his being nicknames the Yellow Earl. A sports fanatic, he was dubbed England's Greatest Sporting Gentleman

and was the founding member and first president of the National Sporting Club, donating the original Lonsdale Belt (made of gold by Mappin & Webb) for British boxing champions. He was also the founding member of the Automobile Association, a keen foxhunter and briefly served as Chairman at Arsenal Football Club. At the castle he entertained politicians, royalty and, in 1895, the German Kaiser.

Having squandered the family fortune, Hugh sold off portions of his estate, but by 1935 he could no longer afford the upkeep of Lowther Castle and moved to a smaller house. He was the last member of the family to be resident there. The castle was requisitioned during the Second World War and used by a tank regiment. It was returned to the family in 1954 considerably the worse for wear.

As well as inheriting a run-down castle, Lancelot, 6th Earl of Lonsdale (1867–1953) also faced a bill of £25 million to clear debts. He had no choice but to auction off the contents of the house in what was seen as the largest country house sale of the 20th century.

Next in line was the four-times married 7th Earl, James Lowther (1922–2006), a passionate conservationist and avowed socialist, who reluctantly removed the castle roof, thus preserving it as a romantic ruin. He covered the lawns of the once-grand gardens in chicken sheds, erected pig pens, and covered the rest of the estate with a spruce plantation in an effort to preserve what was left of his inheritance.

The Lowther Castle and Gardens Trust was formed in 2005 to oversee the consolidation of the ruin and the restoration of the gardens; both are now open to the public all year round.

LEFT Even without its roof, Lowther Castle is a magnificent place.

FOLLOWING PAGE Lowther Castle's architect, Robert Smirke, went on to design the Royal Opera House.

HAREWOOD CASTLE, WEST YORKSHIRE

In 1797 J. M. W. Turner, and his fellow watercolourist Thomas Girton, completed a series of studies of the abandoned ruins of Harewood Castle. They had been commissioned by their patron Edward, Viscount Lascelles, who paid Turner 10 guineas for each piece, and Girton, whose work he regarded as superior, 20 guineas for each piece. The pair's subsequent paintings reveal the aesthetic regard the Lascelles family had for this ruinous castle that lies in the grounds of their vast estate.

Harewood Castle was constructed in the mid-14th century by Sir William de Aldeburgh (c.1322–91) the newly appointed Lord of the Manor of Harewood, who was granted a licence to crenellate by the King Edward III in 1366. Earthworks indicate that there were already buildings on the site, but Sir William wanted something brand new to reflect his elevated status, and so demolished what was there and started afresh.

The building was essentially a fortified tower house, rather than a castle, offering the family protection and providing a substantial hillside home that could be seen for miles around, with views across Wharfedale. Within the thick walls of the house were numerous floors, and while the four towers, portcullis and narrow arrow-slit windows indicate its defensive attributes, the mullioned windows and chapel reveal a desire to create a pleasant home environment and hint at the family's wealth and power.

On the death of de Aldeburgh's only son in 1391, ownership of the castle was split between Sir William's two daughters Sybil Ryther and Elizabeth Redmayne, and subsequently shared for the next two centuries by their husbands' families. James Ryther (1536–95) bought out the Redmayne side of the family in 1574, but this may have been an extravagance too many as he was later imprisoned for debt in both 1592 and in 1594. He appears to have been a deeply unpopular man who was separately described as 'a sour and sallow papist' and 'a man profoundly studied in Machiavelli'. Following his death in 1595 the castle was put up for sale to clear his debts. After passing through the hands of various owners the castle was sold to Henry Lascelles (1690–1753) as part of the Harewood and Gawthorpe estate. Lascelles' son Edwin, 1st Baron Harewood, commissioned the construction of Harewood House between 1759 and 1771. The grounds, designed by Lancelot 'Capability' Brown, utilised the castle as a picturesque ruin.

In 2000 a £1 million restoration project, funded by the Harewood Estate and English Heritage, undertook essential repair and consolidation works, and in 2008 Harewood Castle was taken off the Buildings at Risk register. Harewood Castle still stands proud and can be seen on visits to Harewood House.

RIGHT Harewood Castle lies in the grounds of Harewood House and was utilised by Capability Brown as part of the landscaping design.

WALES

WALES

- MANCHESTER
- BIRMINGHAM
- CARDIFF
- BRISTOL

LEFT The portcullis at Caerphilly Castle.

PREVIOUS PAGE Carreg Cennen Castle sits high in the Brecon Beacons.

1. TINTERN ABBEY
2. PONT Y PANDY SLATE MILL
3. DOLAUCOTHI GOLD MINES
4. CAERPHILLY CASTLE
5. CARREG CENNEN CASTLE
6. BEAUMARIS CASTLE

The title of 'First Colony' is debated between the Irish and the Welsh, but the Normans invaded Wales just shy of century before they moved into Ireland. The Romans came before them in AD48, followed by the Vikings, who plundered religious houses, and then finally those serial builders of castles, the Normans, or as they later became known – the English. The Romans left behind a scattering of coins, a fort in Caerleon and gold mines in Dolaucothi (see pages 120–123). William I and his descendants, notably Edward I, left behind great glowering fortresses, thrown up at speed to deal with any local threat. The all-powerful Marcher Lords, the King's representatives in Wales, rampaged through the country, controlling and repressing the local population. The Welsh were eventually denied the right to own land, bear arms, educate their children or hold senior office, though it is said that the English never conquered Wales over 600ft, where the armoured knights lost the advantage over the fleet-footed Welsh archers. Colonial exploitation continued with the coming of the Industrial Revolution and the land was systematically pillaged on a grand scale for its stone and minerals. The principality became one giant quarry or mine, and bar a few notable exceptions, all had English proprietors. Coal, slate, copper, tin, gold and stone were stripped out, leaving a land scarred with haunting industrial ruins.

TINTERN ABBEY, MONMOUTHSHIRE

The Cistercian Roman Catholic Order was born in 1098, when a small group of monks established a breakaway movement in Cîteaux, near Dijon in Burgundy, France, aiming to follow more rigorous standards of religious observance than were being practised in other wealthy and worldly abbeys. Dubbed the 'White Monks' for their white wool habits, they followed a daily programme of liturgy, manual labour and reading that strictly adhered to the rules of St Benedict.

The movement grew exponentially over the course of 50 years with some 300 Cistercian monasteries springing up across Europe during this relatively short period. The first in the UK was Waverley in England in 1128, the second was Tintern Abbey in Wales, which was founded just three years later in 1131. Walter de Clare, Lord of Chepstow donated the land in the Wye Valley, and a group of monks from L'Aumone in France were sent to Wales to establish the order in Tintern, initially living and worshipping in hastily assembled timber buildings. By the middle of the 12th century the monks and lay brothers had constructed a stone church and cloisters, but the success of the order and its rapid growth necessitated construction on a larger scale.

The 5th Earl of Norfolk, the aptly-named Roger Bigod (c.1245–1306), was determined to establish a place for himself in heaven by acting as patron to Tintern Abbey. It was in part his finances that enabled the monks to rebuild a much larger second church slightly to the north of the original. Work commenced in 1269, and the new Gothic abbey was consecrated in 1301. It is the ruins of this building that still stand in the Wye Valley, though the foundations of the first church can still be seen. In its heyday it was home to around 400 monks and lay brothers who farmed the church estates.

The first case of the Black Death in Wales was recorded in April 1349. Customs collectors in Carmarthen were early victims, and from there the plague spread rapidly across Wales. Tintern, together with other religious communities, was badly affected as the monks did not shirk from treating the sick in their infirmaries, thus spreading the plague to their brethren. By the end of the 14th century it was estimated that 100,000 people had died of the plague in Wales, the population was reduced by one-third to 200,000. Tintern Abbey was no longer able to farm its vast estates and for a time the Abbey had to lease out its lands for others to work. The Abbey itself sat on 11ha (27 acres) of land and the monks not only farmed efficiently following sound practices, but developed fisheries and built mills, turning their land into a prosperous estate.

Henry VIII's Act of Supremacy (1534) separated England and Wales from Papal authority and made the King the Supreme Head of the Church of England. It also enabled Henry to seize control of the religious houses, which were reputed to own a quarter of the country's landed wealth. Tintern, the wealthiest abbey in Wales, was handed over to the Crown in September 1536, and the site was granted to the Earl of Worcester, Henry Somerset. He stripped the lead from the roofs and leased out the land in small parcels; makeshift homes sprang up on Abbey land and the existing buildings were converted into dwellings. From this date Tintern Abbey was left to fall into a ruinous state, with plants colonising the brickwork and ivy steadily creeping up over the walls.

Tintern Abbey was consecrated in 1301, and it is the ruins of this church that still stand.

Change came in the form of domestic tourism – the Wye Valley has been described as the birthplace of British tourism. This was fuelled by the French Revolution (1789–99), which impeded safe foreign travel, and by the improving infrastructure in Britain in the late 17th and 18th centuries. (It was in 1798 that Wordsworth wrote his famous 'Lines written a few miles above Tintern Abbey'.) In the Wye Valley not only was the scenery picturesque and varied, but for the English visitor travelling to Wales it still had some of the allure of foreign travel. Reaching the ruins of Tintern Abbey was a challenge – the roads in the vicinity were poor, even on horseback – but beginning in the 1740s, river trips along the Wye formed the start of the burgeoning tourist industry.

The Abbey remained in the hands of the Earls of Worcester – later Dukes of Beaufort – through the centuries. In 1756 the 5th Duke of Beaufort, Henry Somerset, who had some interest in archaeology ordered excavations at the site, which was cleared. Later the perimeter was fenced and gated and a local steward appointed. In 1901 the Crown Estate purchased the property for its preservation. Ivy was removed from the building and restoration work was started and continued into 1928. Cadw, the Welsh Government's historic environment service, took over management in 1984 and in 2001 the site was Grade I listed.

RIGHT Tintern Abbey has been described as the birthplace of British tourism.

PONT Y PANDY SLATE MILL, GWYNEDD

The soaring ruins of Pont y Pandy loom large in the peaceful Cwmystradllyn Valley in north-west Wales. Yet for eight short years from 1859, this peaceful spot twixt mountain and moorland, was the site of a burgeoning slate mining business.

The production of slate, which was found in large quantities in North Wales, was conducted on a small scale for centuries, hampered by the difficulties of transporting the material from source to the sea where it could be transported cheaply to markets in England, Ireland and France. But as Britain entered the Industrial Revolution, and cities grew exponentially, the demand for slate, and notably roof tiling, greatly increased. By the end of the 18th century ten times the amount of slate was being shipped out from Welsh ports as had been at its start. The material has been utilised since Roman times for its weatherproofing properties and for flooring.

The Gorseddau Quarry, opened in 1807, was a small concern until it was developed by the extravagantly named Bavarian mining engineer Henry Tobias Tschudy von Uster between 1854 and 1857. Development required a huge investment in mining the quarry, the construction of a slate mill – a mighty three-storey structure at Pont y Pandy – transportation, initially by horse-drawn carts, and housing for workers at the village of Treforys. All in all, it was quite an undertaking given that von Uster had been imprisoned for bankruptcy in 1847.

In 1854 the project was taken over by the Victorian entrepreneurs Robert Gill and John Harris who, with a background in railways, invested in developing transportation from the site. The quarry and Pont y Pandy Mill were connected to Porthmadoc by the Gorseddau Tramway in 1857, engineered by Sir James Brunlees, whose professional achievements include the Solway Firth railway viaduct. In 1857, 226 tonnes of slate were despatched, but by 1859 some 200 men were hard at work producing 1,400 tonnes of slate per year between them; output peaked in 1860 with 2,140 tonnes of slate being quarried.

During the mid-19th century the slate industry in north-west Wales boomed. It was a brutal life for the quarrymen who worked in gangs to blast chunks of slate while dangling from ropes and chains on the towering slate terraces. They were paid for the weight of slate produced – poundage – and the quality produced, which could vary according to the seam they had been allocated to work.

From its peak in 1860, slate production in Gorseddau fell to 850 tonnes in 1865, then down to a paltry 25 tonnes in 1867. Despite the investment in the mill, the machinery, the tramway and the housing, there simply was not enough good-quality slate at the site to make the project viable. The Bangor and Porthmadoc Slate Company went into liquidation in 1871. The mill was abandoned, and the quarrymen and their families left the village to seek a living elsewhere. Today the ruins of Gorseddau Quarry, complete with its terraces and waste tips, Pont y Pandy Mill, with its tramways and machinery and the village of Treforys, bear witness to a once great industry and the importance of analysing the true worth of an investment venture in advance.

RIGHT The three-storey Pont y Pandy Mill was constructed to meet 19th-century demand for slate.

DOLAUCOTHI GOLD MINES, CARMARTHENSHIRE

Carmarthenshire was the focus of considerable Roman activity from AD74–125, and the quest for gold was the lure. On their departure little remained but a curiously sculpted landscape, and local tales of the presence of gold. A haul of gold jewellery discovered by a farmer in 1797 revived interest, but it was not until the year 2000 that archaeological research finally confirmed that gold had been extracted from this area, possibly as far back as the Bronze Age.

The Johnes family, who had been in possession of the Dolaucothi Estate since the 16th century, took an active interest in the heritage of the area. In 1767 they were visited by the botanist Joseph Banks (1743-1820), who wanted to see the leat he had heard talk of at Dolaucothi. Banks described the Caves of 'Gogofa', as the locals called the mines, as 'the most wonderful remains of the Ancients that this island affords'. Twenty-two years later he was excited to learn about the discovery of gold jewellery (now in the British Museum), recommending the offer of a reward for any other items recovered.

The Johnes family, who had interests in silver-lead mines in Cardiganshire, were keen to discover if there was still any gold in their land. In the 1780s they leased the mines to one Chauncy Townsend, a coal and copper magnate, but nothing of value was found. The study of antiquarian relics was fashionable amongst the wealthy and Judge John Johnes (1800–76) worked assiduously in his time at Dolaucothi to uncover the

LEFT An old mining tub at Dolaucothi Gold Mines. The horizontal line on the hill is the remains of a Roman leat (aqueduct) used by the Romans to flush out gold.

story behind the mysterious mines on his estate, inviting experts down to examine relics and the caves.

In 1823 the Judge, who later met an untimely end after being shot and killed by his own butler, advertised the mines as for lease, 'unworked since Roman times'. A geological survey of the area undertaken by Henry de la Beche in 1844 was enlivened by his claim to have found gold, though only a minute particle. In 1871 commercial mining was instigated to loud fanfare, quartz-crushing machinery was installed and some gold was found, but by 1879 the site was abandoned.

The Gold Rushes in California and South Africa reignited interest and the Johnes family leased out the mine once more, but this venture collapsed in 1894. A series of other interested parties and investors leased the mine hoping to strike it rich. In 1905 the mine actually made a rare and small profit of £172 – but all ventures were ultimately to fail. The final efforts were abandoned in 1939 with the threat of war.

The Dolaucothi Estate was bequeathed to the National Trust in 1941 by relatives of the Johnes family. Work was undertaken to clear tunnels and drain flooded sections of the mine and tours began in 1983. In 1999 National Trust began to run the site as a visitor attraction, allowing visitors to see for themselves the remains of the local gold industry, from the Roman mines to the heavier industry of the 1930s.

RIGHT Remains of the old 1930s mine buildings at Dolaucothi.

CAERPHILLY CASTLE, CAERPHILLY

The largest castle in Wales, and indeed the second largest in the UK – only Windsor is bigger – Caerphilly Castle was built in just three years. Its cutting-edge concentric design made it virtually impregnable, though shifts in politics rendered its purpose redundant soon after completion.

The fortress was constructed by the bombastic Gilbert de Clare (1243–95). One of the wealthiest and most powerful English Marcher Lords, de Clare was not averse to conflict. Dubbed 'Gilbert the Red' because of the colour of his hair, he picked quarrels with King Henry III, Pope Clement IV, his neighbour Humphrey de Bohun, his first wife Alice de Lusignan, whom he divorced, and the sovereign Prince of Wales, Llywelyn ap Gruffydd (c.1223–82).

In 1263, at the tender age of 20, Gilbert the Red took charge of the family estate, seeking to halt the advances of Llywelyn, who had taken advantage of the war between Henry III and his rebel barons to expand his hold on the county of Glamorgan. Gilbert advanced north from Cardiff and built Caerphilly Castle to reinforce his position and prevent Llywelyn's advances south from his stronghold in Mid and North Wales.

Work began apace in April 1268 and Llywelyn, who was at this time on good terms with the English King, attacked the castle, burning timbers to halt progress. Henry III intervened and advised Gilbert to abandon his scheme, but the Marcher Lord paid no attention and redoubled his construction efforts. Built on a 12ha (30-acre) site on a natural spur of land, this medieval fortress was inspired by Kenilworth Castle's cutting-edge

RIGHT
Surrounded by a series of moats, Caerphilly Castle sits on an artificial island.

126 Wales

concentric walls with fortified gatehouses. This imposing edifice had few windows and little in the way of decoration, further reinforcing its strength.

Beyond it, the Nant y Gledyr stream was dammed, creating an artificial lake that ringed this new island. The water prevented the castle walls being undermined in siege, and naturally impeded the range of military throwing machines. The town of Caerphilly grew up alongside, but as it was situated outside the castle walls it was left vulnerable to attack.

After the death of Henry III, Llywelyn lost patience with his successor, Edward I (1239–1307), leading to two Welsh campaigns for independence. Edward defeated Llywelyn in 1277, annexed the principality and built a ring of castles, including Beaumaris, Caernarfon, Harlech and Conwy. He evicted Welsh peasants and imported thousands of English settlers. In Welsh uprisings against Royal officers in 1287 and 1294, large parts of Caerphilly town were burnt to the ground, though the great fortress proved impossible to conquer.

Following Gilbert's death, and the death of his son, also Gilbert, on the first day of fighting in the Battle of Bannockburn (1314), the castle had a succession of custodians. Hugh Despenser 'the Younger', who had married Eleanor de Clare, Gilbert's sister, was a favourite of Edward II, and reputedly his lover. In

1326 when the King's wife, Queen Isabella, sought to depose her husband with a view to making her son regent, the King and Despenser fled to Caerphilly Castle and on to Llantrisant where both were captured.

Despenser suffered a brutal public execution, while the King was forced to abdicate in favour of his son, Edward III.

As tensions with the Welsh eased in the 15th century Caerphilly Castle became redundant, and by 1538 it was described as ruinous. The castle's owner, Henry Herbert Earl of Pembroke, utilised its stone to construct a house nearby. The leaning south-east tower is said to have been due to 'slighting' by Oliver Cromwell's troops in the English Civil War (1642–51) to ensure that the castle could no longer be used as an effective fortification, but it could also have been caused by subsidence.

In 1766 Caerphilly Castle was acquired by John Stewart, 4th Earl of Bute, on his marriage to Charlotte Hickman Windsor, whose family had vast estates in South Wales. His son, the 2nd Marquess of Bute realised the potential of the South Wales coalfields and constructed Cardiff Docks, building up a large fortune in the process. Subsequent generations of his family used this fortune to help preserve and restore Caerphilly Castle, and in 1950 the 5th Marquess of Bute, John Crichton Stuart, gave the castle to the state. Today it is protected by Cadw.

FAR LEFT The imposing gatehouse entrance helped deter invaders.

LEFT Arrow slit in the wall of Caerphilly Castle, allowing the archer inside to vary the elevation of his shots.

CARREG CENNEN CASTLE, CARMARTHENSHIRE

Perched high on a crag, the weather-beaten ruins of Castell Carreg Cennen ('Castle on the Rock') overlook the Black Mountains and the River Cennen, in what is now Brecon Beacons National Park. Boasting what an estate agent would call a spectacular location, this defensive fortress of a castle is protected on two sides by a 30.5m (100ft) limestone cliff, and on the north and east sides by a series of dastardly pits, drawbridges and gatehouses, all with the military advantage of panoramic views in every direction.

This defensive position may previously have been utilised by the Romans – Roman coins were found here – and archaeological evidence shows an even earlier presence: three skeletons dating from the Upper Palaeolithic era were discovered in a cave. It was not until the 12th century, however, that the Welsh Princes recognised the value of this site's strategic position. Rhys ap Gruffydd (1132–97) is credited with erecting the first castle on the site. It was one of a series he built in Wales following a rapprochement with the English king Henry II after many years of fighting over his royal rank and land rights.

The castle remained in Welsh hands for almost a century until 1283 when it was taken by the English during the first War of Welsh Independence and granted to the King's man John Giffard (1232–99). This English nobleman is credited with rebuilding it in the form we see today, although in practice he probably spent little time there and merely funded the works.

The one fault in the design concerned the water supply. Aside from the water cisterns that collected rainwater inside the castle, the principal source of water was a clay-lined ditch outside the castle, which left the fortress vulnerable to siege. This fact has led to some debate as to whether Carreg Cennen is Welsh or English in design – the English favoured internal water supplies.

The castle is home to an extraordinary vaulted passage that runs deep beneath the castle, leading to a cave. There has been some speculation as to its purpose. It was certainly home to dove-houses; the young – squabs – would have been a food source, and according to folklore, the passage led to an additional water supply. However, the very existence of such a tunnel left the castle vulnerable to breaching, even though the mouth of the cave was blocked.

John Gifford's son – also John – joined the Baron's uprising of 1321 against Henry II's favourite Hugh Despenser and was executed, whereupon the castle was handed over to the care of Despenser, later passing into the hands of John of Gaunt and becoming part of the vast estates of the Duchy of Lancaster. It was thus acquired by his son, Henry Bolingbroke, later Henry IV, forming a doomed link with the House of Lancaster.

In July 1403 Owain Glyndwr – the self-proclaimed Prince of Wales and the last Welshman to hold the title – lay siege to Carreg Cennen for several months in the Glyndwr Rising (1400–15). The Welsh had supported King Richard II and Glyndwr rose against Henry IV following a dispute, engaging in hit-and-run guerrilla tactics against the English and liberating castles from English rule. Henry enacted punitive legislation against the Welsh, preventing them from buying land, holding

senior office, bearing arms or being educated. These actions only fuelled the movement to free Wales. Carreg Cennen did not fall under siege, but withstanding this onslaught took its toll. Glyndwr's campaigns continued until 1406 but then faltered.

In 1455 Carreg Cennen's owner, Gruffudd ap Nicholas, undertook reinforcement. A Lancastrian supporter, Gruffudd's stronghold was used by Lancastrian forces as a convenient bolthole during the Wars of the Roses (1455–85). He fought in the Battle of Mortimer Cross in Herefordshire in February 1461, in which the Welsh Lancastrian supporters, led by Owen and his son Jasper Tudor, the Earl of Pembroke, were defeated and thus were prevented from joining forces with the main Lancastrian army that was marching on London.

Owen Tudor was pursued, caught and beheaded by Yorkists. Gruffudd fled with his troops to Carreg Cennen. In 1462 Sir William Herbert and Sir Roger Vaughan took the castle for the Yorkists, and a troop of 500 men set about destroying the castle with crowbars and picks to prevent it from ever being used against them again. What was left of the castle was handed to Sir Rhys ap Thomas by Henry VII, and it later came under the ownership of the Earls of Cawdor. Today the castle is owned by a local farmer, who acquired it as part of his farm, and the site is managed by Cadw.

LEFT Owain Glyndwr laid siege to Carreg Cennen in the movement to free Wales.

BEAUMARIS CASTLE, ANGLESEY

Edward I (1239–1307) built or rebuilt an impressive number of castles in the principality of Wales – eight in total – spending some £173,000 in 35 years on the throne. He also captured four castles from the Welsh and repaired those too, an average that works out at around one castle for every three years of his reign.

Edward had put down a rebellion by Llywelyn ap Gruffydd in 1277, and a more forceful national campaign in 1282–33 by Llywelyn's brother Dafydd. This time Edward set out to conquer Wales. Following his victory, he began a programme of colonisation and settlement and built a series of castles to form a ring of stone around North Wales. Beaumaris Castle on Anglesey was the last castle he commissioned. Work began in the summer of 1295, but was never actually completed.

Beaumaris Castle, which overlooks the Menai Straits, is regarded as the loveliest of all Edward's castles. Like the others, its construction was supervised by the Master of Royal Works in Wales, James of St George, the greatest military engineer of the age.

The castle was erected at speed: Master James employed 2,600 men in the first year of construction alone. Beaumaris was concentric in design with a stout outer curtain wall with 12 semicircular towers, ringing a taller inner castle with six huge round towers and two twin-towered gatehouses. The outer wall is ringed by a moat, with a tidal dock for shipping on the south side. On 12 February 1296, a little under a year after work had started, Master James wrote to the Treasurer and Barons of the Exchequer at Westminster, pleading for more money to complete works on the castle, his letter survives and is kept in the Royal Archives at Kew.

The castle was equipped with state apartments, a chapel, murder holes, stone gargoyles, and had patterned stone work, but work slowed with each passing year and had ceased completely by 1300. Despite the vast expense, Beaumaris was put to very little practical use. Owain Glyndwr lay siege to it in 1403 and took it but Beaumaris was reclaimed by Henry IV's forces in 1405. By the 16th century it was in a state of poor repair and guarded by just eight to ten guns and 40 bowmen.

The castle's strategic position assumed fresh significance during the English Civil War (1642–51), as it was able to provide an essential link between the King's forces in Ireland and operations in England. It was managed at the time by Thomas Bulkeley who led the King's forces in Anglesey. When Cromwell's forces defeated Royalist armies in 1646 Bulkeley surrendered the castle to Parliament, but when Charles II (1630–85) was restored to the throne in 1660, he returned Beaumaris to the care of the Bulkeley family.

In 1925 Beaumaris Castle was handed back to the state and is now in the care of Cadw. Today it is a UNESCO-listed World Heritage Site, said to be one of the finest examples of 13th- and 14th-century military architecture in Europe.

RIGHT Beaumaris Castle was the last Welsh castle commissioned by Edward I.

NORTHERN IRELAND

NORTHERN IRELAND

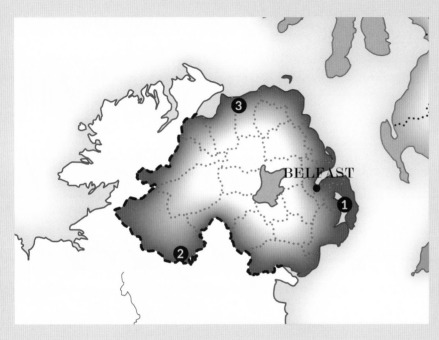

LEFT The view from Old Castle Crom to Crichton Tower on God Island, built around 1847.

PREVIOUS PAGE Downhill Demesne was constructed for the Earl-Bishop Dr Frederick Hervey.

1 GREY ABBEY
2 OLD CASTLE CROM
3 DOWNHILL DEMESNE

The ruins of Northern Ireland highlight the region's history of occupation and colonisation. Commissioned not by the Irish themselves, but by Norman invaders, English, Welsh or Scottish 'planters', and the English ruling classes, they are permanent reminders of the repression of the Irish people. The planters were despatched by the English Crown en masse in the 16th and 17th centuries to settle the region. This colonisation, designed to dilute national resistance and make the native Irish more malleable, indelibly marked the region. The influx was so overwhelming that it even influenced the development of the region's distinctive twang. Old Crom Castle (see pages 140–141), a tower house with fortified barn, was built by a Scottish planter. He was wise to fortify as the locals were not best pleased to have their land snatched by incomers. In the 13th century, Affreca, a princess from the Kingdom of Man and the Scottish Isles and the bride of a Norman mercenary soldier, graciously founded Grey Abbey in County Down. As in Wales, Gaelic speakers were not allowed to hold official posts. Instead, these went to English or Anglo-Irish candidates. The Rt Rev. Dr Frederick Hervey, Bishop of Derry, a flamboyant English cleric, was one such incumbent. Hervey utilised church lands to build Downhill Demesne (see pages 142–147), but at least he had the good grace to rail against the English government's treatment of Irish Catholics, as well as working to improve the infrastructure and alleviate poverty.

GREY ABBEY, COUNTY DOWN

Lying on the Ards Peninsula that separates Strangford Lough from the Straits of Moyle is Grey Abbey, a reminder of the impact that the Norman conquest had on the area.

This area of County Down in Northern Ireland was conquered by the Normans in the 12th century, and Somerset-born John de Courcy was among their number. The Norman forces were mercenaries employed by Diarmaid Mac Murchadha to help him regain his position as King of Leinster. In 1177, without the permission of King Henry II, de Courcy overthrew the last King of Ulaid (Ulster), built himself a castle at Carrickfergus and made a political match with Affreca, the daughter of the King of Man and the Isles, Godred Olafsson. As the second son with no claim on his family's estates, de Courcy clearly wanted to carve a niche for himself and helped himself to a large chunk of Ulster.

Affreca founded Grey Abbey in 1193. As a noblewoman of the Crovan dynasty of Gaelic Scandinavian origin, she was hardly a local. Legend has it that Affreca's magnanimity in building the Abbey was prompted by a safe landing after a perilous sea voyage. This stone-built Cistercian monastery, a daughter house of Holmcultram Abbey in Cumbria, was the first Gothic design in Ulster. At its height the community here numbered just 40–50 monks. King John exiled de Courcy from Ireland in 1205, and Affreca's patronage of the Grey Abbey ended.

Around 1315 the Abbey was almost destroyed by Edward Bruce, younger brother of Robert the Bruce, who supported the Irish struggle to free the country from English control. It must have recovered sufficiently for Henry VIII to dissolve it in 1541, though it was in a poor state of repair. Nevertheless, Brian O'Neill set it alight in 1572 to prevent it being used as a refuge by English colonists, though he later had to concede the land to the Ulster-Scots.

In 1626 the ruins of the Abbey were granted to Sir Hugh Montgomery, 1st Viscount Montgomery of the Great Ards (1560–1636). An early settler from Scotland in 1606, and one of the founding fathers of the Ulster-Scots, he had Grey Abbey rebuilt and reroofed in 1626 and it served as a parish church for another 150 years until a new church was built. The Abbey graveyard is home to a number of tombstones for the Montgomery family who still own nearby Grey Abbey House and its estate. The ruins are currently maintained by the Northern Ireland Environment Agency.

RIGHT Grey Abbey was founded in the late 12th century by Affreca, the daughter of the King of Man and the Isles.

OLD CASTLE CROM, COUNTY FERMANAGH

On the shores of Upper Lough Erne are two conjoined yew trees that were described as venerable as far back as 1734. Reputed to be over 1,000 years old, they sit beside the ruins of Old Castle Crom – pronounced 'crumb' – whose remains highlight the impact of England's policy of Irish colonisation after brutal years of conflict.

Throughout the Tudor period the English government sought to eliminate the risk of invasion and rebellion from Ireland. The Nine Years' War (1593–1603) between England and Ireland saw the Irish rebellion put down. Elizabeth I's English forces used a scorched-earth military strategy in Ulster, burning corn, destroying crops, and killing or driving cattle to induce a terrible famine. England was very nearly bankrupted by the cost of the conflict, and more mindful of the Crown's finances following his accession in 1603, James I (1566–1625) decided to pursue a more robust policy of colonisation to gain control of Ireland peacefully and quietly inculcate English and Scottish culture and religion in what became known as the Ulster Plantation.

Scottish and English protestants were despatched to Ulster; it is estimated that by the first half of the century some 100,000 Scots – who would have spoken neither Gaelic nor English – and 20,000 English had settled this region. This was not a project to embark on lightly as settlers were often massacred by disgruntled Irish Catholics. As a policy it only served to fuel religious differences and heighten sectarian bitterness, sowing the seeds of disquiet for long years to come.

Old Castle Crom was built in the early 17th century by Scottish Planter Michael Balfour. It consisted of a tower house with a 'bawn' or fortified barn to keep both cattle and the inhabitants safe from raiders. It was clearly not a happy experience for Balfour, and Crom was sold within ten years.

In 1655 the castle came into the hands of the Creighton (later Crichton) family who hailed from Scotland but had settled in Ireland. In 1685 David Creighton twice defended the family seat against the Jacobite army, retaining the family home. Having survived this struggle it was badly damaged by a domestic fire in 1764.

Quite where the family lived for the next 50 years is a matter of speculation, but John Crichton, the 3rd Earl Erne and one of the original Irish Representative Peers in the House of Lords, planned a grand comeback. The new Castle Crom, completed around 1838, was designed by Edward Blore, the same architect responsible for Buckingham Palace (he took over after John Nash was dismissed) and cost a cool £29,000. The ruin of Old Castle Crom was retained, with additional walls and towers added in the 19th century to heighten its picturesque effect.

Crom Castle remains with the Earls of Erne today, but its estate and Old Castle Crom were handed to the management of the National Trust in 1987.

LEFT Old Castle Crom was constructed by a Scottish planter in the early 17th century.

DOWNHILL DEMESNE, COUNTY LONDONDERRY

Standing on an exposed Atlantic headland, just 122m (400ft) away from the sea, are the ruins of the once-great mansion, Downhill Demesne. It was designed for the flamboyant Dr Frederick Hervey (1730–1803), otherwise known as the Earl-Bishop for his twin titles of Bishop of Derry and 4th Earl of Bristol.

As the third son, young Hervey had no prospect of a title, so he studied law at Cambridge, was ordained in 1754 and appointed Royal Chaplain in 1763; George III referred to him as 'that wicked prelate'. A linguist with an appetite for food, drink, art, travel and conversation, he corresponded regularly with such luminaries as Benjamin Franklin, Goethe, James Boswell, the Pope and Voltaire, who observed: 'when God created the human race he made men, women and Herveys.'

Another passion was volcanology and while Hervey could not claim to have discovered Giant's Causeway, he was certainly one of the first to write about it extensively, which led to the Royal Society making him a Fellow. He found the headland location for Downhill on rides to Giant's Causeway and decided to build his great house there. Having inherited his brother's title and an annual income of £20,000 a year he now had the funds at his disposal to build his dream house and to collect art.

The Cork-born architect Michael Shanahan was commissioned to design the house in the early 1770s. One wing housed an art gallery with paintings by Titian, Raphael and Tintoretto. The grounds were

RIGHT The south front of the ruins of Downhill House. The house was built around 1774 for the Earl Bishop Frederick Hervey.

FOLLOWING PAGE The ruins of Downhill House seen from the west front.

dotted with extraordinary buildings; the Mussenden Temple, which stands at the very edge of the cliff, served as an overflow library and was named after Hervey's cousin Frideswide Mussenden, of whom he was excessively fond. It was modelled on the Temple of Vesta in Tivoli. Naturally Hervey had tried to buy the real thing, but was rebuffed.

A contemporary of Hervey's observed that the house was built where only a romantic would expect to find one and only a lunatic would build one. Another visitor noted that in a storm the servants had to practically crawl on hands and knees to get across the courtyard. No wonder Downhill was not Hervey's main home – that was the ancestral family seat at Ickworth in Surrey, where his wife chose to spend most of her time.

A flamboyant dresser and great eccentric, as Bishop he was said to make his curates race along the beach to obtain a promotion. Hervey was also a philanthropist who built roads and tried to alleviate the poverty of the area. He promoted religious tolerance and raged against the English treatment of Irish Catholics. Hervey died on his release from prison in Italy; the French had held him in Milan for 18 months for spying. In typically flamboyant fashion he asked for his body to be sent home in a cask of sherry. Hervey did not leave Downhill to his family, but to a cousin once removed, the Rev. Henry Bruce.

Downhill was almost gutted by fire in 1851. The Bruce family restored the house from 1870–74 and continued to live there until 1923. The house was requisitioned by the Air Ministry in 1941, which remained there until the end of the Second World War. Sir Hervey Bruce sold Downhill in 1946 and the new owner later dismantled the house, leaving behind a substantial ruin, which continues to dominate the landscape for many miles around to this day. The ruin of Downhill came into National Trust care in 1980 and the Trust provides ongoing public access to this most unique site.

RIGHT Italian stuccadores were employed to create the decorative carving on the house.

FAR RIGHT Hervey named Mussenden Temple after his beloved cousin.

SCOTLAND

SCOTLAND

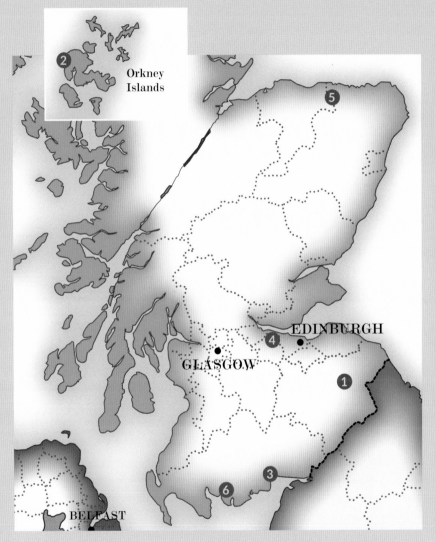

Orkney Islands

EDINBURGH
GLASGOW
BELFAST

In the whole of the United Kingdom, Scotland is home to the oldest ruin of all: the beautifully preserved Neolithic village of Skara Brae (see pages 156–157), which dates back to 3100BC. Perfectly preserved in a tomb of sand, it fared rather better than many of Scotland's other great buildings, which were repeatedly battered by conflict. The country is liberally peppered with ruined tower houses, such as Cardoness Castle (see pages 168–169), for it was advisable to live in a state of constant fortification. Not only was there regular inter-clan fighting, but also repeated tussles over who should sit on the throne of Scotland, as well as the protracted struggle with English invaders. The clans kept a watchful eye on the balance of power and a whisper in the royal ear could bring about a calamitous fall from grace that saw your castle burned to the ground and your estates confiscated. A punitive attack on property was often the first stage of a royal ticking off! The picturesque border country was hardest hit, and even Melrose Abbey (see pages 152–155) was repeatedly attacked. The latter eventually succumbed to the Scottish Reformation, which saw Scotland break with Rome. Though rather gentler in approach than the asset-stripping of the Dissolution of the Monasteries in England and Wales of 1536–1541; it nevertheless led to the ruin of many beautiful religious institutions.

1 MELROSE ABBEY
2 SKARA BRAE
3 SWEETHEART ABBEY
4 LINLITHGOW PALACE
5 HUNTLY CASTLE
6 CARDONESS CASTLE

LEFT The interior of Neolithic House 1 at Skara Brae.

PREVIOUS PAGE Melrose Abbey was Scotland's first Cistercian monastery and it was founded by King David I of Scotland in 1136.

MELROSE ABBEY, ROXBURGHSHIRE

In 1996, a group of archaeologists tried to uncover the truth behind the story that the heart of Robert I of Scotland (Robert the Bruce) was buried at Melrose Abbey. The casket they unearthed was moved to an Edinburgh laboratory for analysis. A small hole was drilled into it so that the contents could be seen via a tiny camera. What they found inside was a small lead container, pitted with age, complete with an engraved copper plaque which read: 'The enclosed leaden casket containing a heart was found beneath Chapter House floor, March 1921, by His Majesty's Office of Works.'

The team thus concluded that although it was not possible to prove with certainty that this was the heart of Robert the Bruce, they could reasonably assume that it was, given that no other records existed of anyone else's heart being buried in the Abbey.

The casket was reinterred at Melrose Abbey ruins on 22 June 1998, 684 years to the day since Bruce's decisive victory over the English at the Battle of Bannockburn in the First War of Scottish Independence in 1314. The spot in the ruins where his heart now lies has been marked with a plinth. Robert I's body, *sans* heart, had been buried at Dunfermline Abbey, but it is said that he requested his heart be removed on his death and taken on crusade. The orders were followed by one James Douglas, Robert's friend and supporter, who died on

RIGHT The heart of Robert the Bruce is buried at Melrose Abbey.

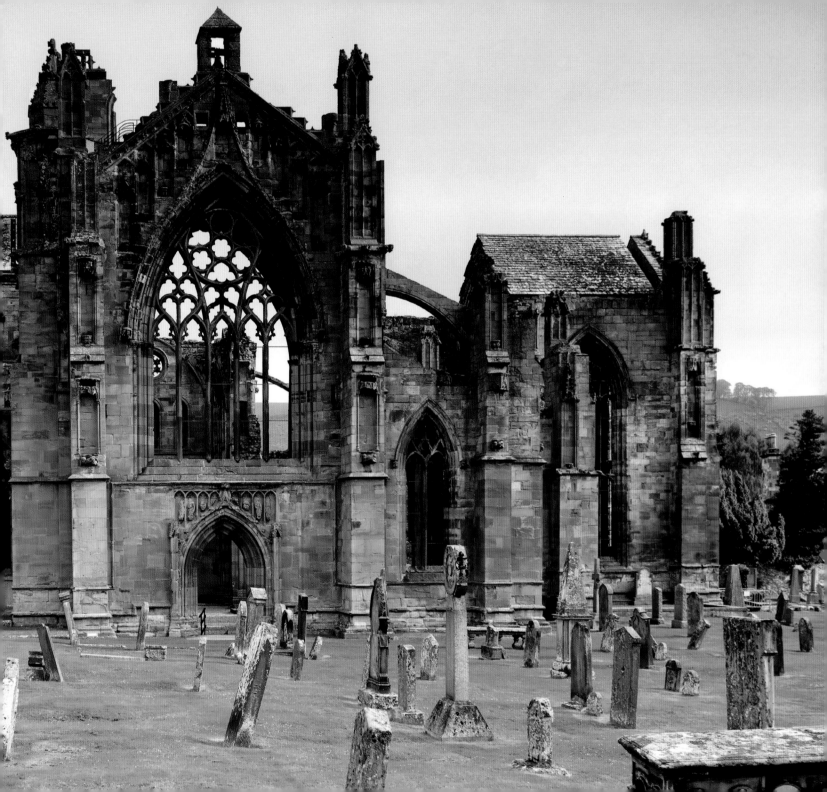

this mission, but the King's heart was reputedly retrieved and returned to Melrose for burial.

St Aidan founded a monastery at Old Melrose in AD650, but this was destroyed in 839 by Kenneth MacAlpin, later King of the Picts. King David I sought to establish a new Cistercian monastery on the same site in 1136, but the monks argued that farmland a few miles west would prove a more propitious spot. Melrose Abbey was duly founded there. Monks from Rievaulx Abbey in Yorkshire came to help with the construction, and in just ten years the east end of the church was complete and a service of dedication was held, though construction work continued for the next 50 years.

What the monks hadn't anticipated was that their idyllic border country location saw Melrose Abbey repeatedly caught up in the fractious relationship between the English and the Scots. It was partially destroyed in 1322 by Edward II and his army, and many monks were killed. Robert the Bruce funded its reconstruction, thus establishing his connection with the Abbey. But in 1385, after a Scots invasion of northern England, Richard II pursued the retreating Scots past Melrose Abbey and had it burned to the ground in a fit of pique. Suitably repentant, Richard did begin a programme of reconstruction by way of an apology, and this work was continued by the Scots over the next 100 years.

Existing structures were retained where feasible, but the later design was influenced by European architecture so that the Abbey evolved into an interesting cocktail of ecclesiastical styles. Unfortunately, tensions came to a head again in 1544 and 1545, and the Abbey was a casualty in the futile 'Rough Wooing' campaign. Henry VIII's show of force, designed to convince the Scots that the infant Queen of Scots should be betrothed to his son Prince Edward, spectacularly backfired and thrust her into the arms of the French.

Melrose Abbey never fully recovered from this last assault, and by 1556 the remaining monks were complaining that they could not survive another winter in Melrose. The Scottish Reformation of 1560 marked its death knell, though the existing monks were allowed to remain. By the time the last monk died in 1590, enterprising locals were helping themselves to the Abbey's stone, lead, glass and timber for use elsewhere. The former monks' choir was put to use as a parish church from 1610 and was used as such for the next 200 years. The land was given to the Scotts of Buccleuch and in 1822 their descendant, historical novelist Sir Walter Scott, supervised extensive repair work to preserve the ruins. Melrose Abbey is now under the guardianship of Historic Environment Scotland.

LEFT Melrose Abbey was rebuilt after being largely destroyed by the English in 1385.

SKARA BRAE, ORKNEY

In the winter of 1850, a terrible storm battered the island of Orkney, stripping a large mound of grass and, rather to the surprise of the locals, revealing the outline of several dwellings. This turned out to be a 5,000-year-old Neolithic Settlement, substantially older than the Great Wall of China or even Stonehenge and the Pyramids of Giza.

The local laird, William Watt of Skaill, undertook some amateur excavation of the site, which revealed four ancient, roofless houses. The initial works were abandoned in 1868 and the site left undisturbed until 1913, when a group of 'enterprising' visitors showed up bearing shovels, and happily helped themselves to a number of artefacts. In 1924 more damage was inflicted when another great storm simply swept away part of one of the houses. Finally, before it could be further destroyed by the dual threats of storms and tourists, this fragile site was placed under the guardianship of His Majesty's Commissioners of Works.

Gordon Childe from the University of Edinburgh was charged with heading the work and he travelled to Orkney in 1927 to begin the painstaking excavation, a job he apparently loathed, though his students maintained he was a genius at interpreting evidence. Even Childe could not quite believe what he had found, initially mistakenly dating the village to a mere 500BC.

Eight houses, linked by low covered passages, were uncovered, each perfectly preserved in its tomb of sand, along with quantities of bone, flint tools, grooved pottery and beads. Each house was the same: a square room with central fireplace, furnished with stone beds, a dresser and clay-lined boxes, possibly for water storage or bait. All the furniture was constructed from stone –

given the lack of timber on Orkney, this self-assembly material was suitably robust and readily available. The subterranean design of the huts provided protection from Orkney's brutal elements, and the interconnected covered passageways enabled the inhabitants to move comfortably from hut to hut whatever the weather.

Radiocarbon dating work in the 1970s indicated that the village had been inhabited for around 600 years from 3100BC. The painstaking excavation revealed that the design of the stone huts had evolved, becoming larger and more comfortable with time – it was ever thus. This was not living at its most basic; the villagers went so far as to carve stone balls and whalebone figurines and to hoard beads and whale teeth. They clearly dined on seafood, as evidenced by the fishbones and shells piled up around the houses. It is estimated that the settlement provided accommodation for 50 people at any given time, though why it was abandoned we do not know, nor do we understand why their precious and eminently transportable possessions were left behind to be slowly buried by piles of sand.

The Heart of Neolithic Orkney is a UNESCO-listed site and includes the Ring of Brodgar, a henge and stone circle, the Standing Stones of Stenness, and the burial monument of Maeshowe. It is protected by Historic Environment Scotland.

RIGHT The Neolithic village of Skara Brae lay undiscovered for millennia.

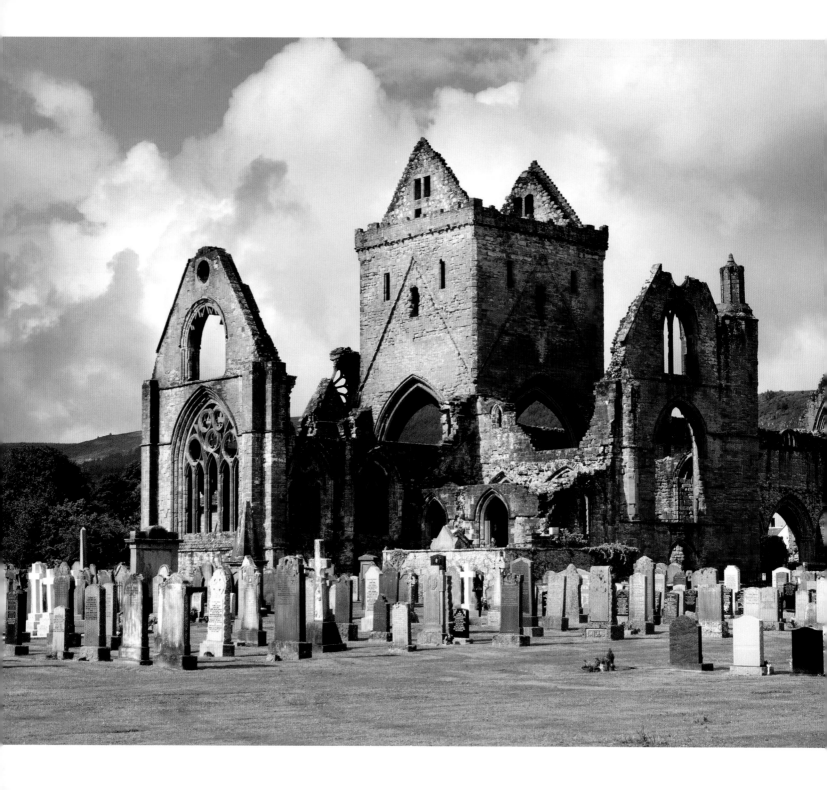

SWEETHEART ABBEY, DUMFRIES AND GALLOWAY

Lady Devorgilla of Galloway (c.1210–90) was a descendant of King David I of Scotland, mother of King John I of Scotland, her youngest child, and grandmother of Edward Balliol, pretender to the Scottish throne. Daughter of the Gaelic Prince Alan of Galloway, Devorgilla was married to John, 5th Baron de Balliol, at the age of 13, and she bore him nine children. On his death in 1269 she had his heart embalmed and placed an ivory casket which she kept with her until her death. The couple are also remembered for founding Balliol College, Oxford.

In 1273 Lady Devorgilla founded New Abbey, Scotland's last Cistercian house, in her husband's memory. Built of warm red sandstone and ringed by a massive precinct wall constructed from granite boulders, it became Lady Devorgilla's final resting place in 1290. In accordance with her wishes she was buried here in front of the high altar, along with the casket containing her husband's heart. This romantic gesture led to New Abbey becoming known as Sweetheart Abbey.

Sweetheart Abbey's days were numbered with the advance of the Protestant Reformation in 1560, but it was saved by one Lord Maxwell, who refused an order by the Lords of the Congregation to demolish the place 'quhair he was maist part brocht up in his youth'. Despite the disposal of the Abbey's assets, it continued to be a place of Catholic worship even after Abbot John Broun retired in 1565. His kinsman Gilbert Broun continued to hold mass here until 1609, in contravention of the law, despite periods of enforced exile in France and imprisonment in Blackness Castle.

In 1624 the Abbey's buildings were utilised by the parish church of Loch Kinder, which moved into the former refectory, thus ensuring the site remained important to the local community as a place of worship and internment. William Paterson, the founder of the Bank of England, was buried here in 1714 and this also contributed to the survival of the ruins.

In the late 18th century plans to remove stone from the Abbey, a fate which had already befallen the chapter house, were halted by a consortium of local men who purchased the land. Their action made Sweetheart Abbey the first medieval ruin to be protected in this way. In 1927 the ruins were put into state care, and it is now under the guardianship of Historic Environment Scotland. Balliol College retains links with Sweetheart Abbey to this day.

LEFT Lady Devorgilla, the founder of Sweetheart Abbey, was so devoted to her husband that after his death she kept his heart in a casket that was later buried with her in the sanctuary here.

LINLITHGOW PALACE, WEST LOTHIAN

The town of Linlithgow lies on the ancient road between Edinburgh and Stirling and the main route north from England making it a site of strategic importance. King David I of Scotland constructed a fortified manor on a tall promontory around 1130, where the Romans are thought to have earlier established a fort. In 1296, Edward I – the Hammer of the Scots – spotted the opportunity to take control of Scotland, as he had already done in Wales, when the Scottish succession crisis in 1287 created a power vacuum. Edward invaded Scotland, deposed the Scottish King John I and sent him to the Tower of London. In the winter of 1301–02 he spent the winter at Linlithgow, reinforcing the manor perimeter and masterminding his invasion of Scotland. As his coffers had been emptied by his Welsh campaigns he could only erect a timber palisade.

After the English defeat at the Battle of Bannockburn (1314) under the command of Robert the Bruce, the Scots pulled the English castle down, retaining the manor, but in 1424 the town, the church and the castle were all attacked in another clash with English forces and burned to the ground.

In response, James I of Scotland set about constructing a grand palace on the site that would reflect his authority. Work ground to a halt after his assassination on 20 February 1437, following a conspiracy by his uncle Walter Stewart, Earl of Atholl. It is estimated that James I spent £7,000 on building Linlithgow Palace – around one-tenth of his income – and the magnificent Great Hall was constructed under

RIGHT James I of Scotland commissioned the construction of Linlithgow Palace.

his watch. Work on the palace continued under the reigns of James III, who added the south range and west range and James IV, who ordered the construction of the north range, enclosing the palace and creating a quadrangle. Linlithgow was given to Margaret Tudor, Henry VII's daughter, as part of her dowry on her marriage to James IV, and later to James V's two French wives, Princess Madeleine (who died of consumption a few months after the wedding) and Mary of Guise, who reputedly described Linlithgow as comparing favourably with the noblest chateaux in France.

James IV used Linlithgow palace regularly; his son James V was born here in 1512, and his daughter, the future Mary Queen of Scots, was born here in 1542. Mary succeeded her father aged just six days and remained at Linlithgow until she was seven months old, when her mother took her to the more secure Stirling Castle. Although she visited Linlithgow on numerous occasions later in life, this was her longest stay here. Mary was whisked away to France at the age of six to escape Henry VIII's 'Rough Wooing'; he wanted her to marry his son Edward and sought to persuade her Scottish advisers by making war.

James VI united the thrones of England and Scotland when he acceded to the throne of England as James I, after the death of Elizabeth I in 1603. He inherited the

palace from his mother, Mary Queen of Scots, but he spent little time there, and the castle was neglected. By the time the north range collapsed in 1607 he had been out of Scotland for four years. Nevertheless, on being informed of its perilous condition, he ordered that the north range be rebuilt, and works were carried out between 1618–1622.

Despite this expenditure he never saw the completed work. The last visit by a reigning monarch was that of Charles I who popped in for a mere day-long visit in 1633.

Oliver Cromwell utilised Linlithgow as a supply base after Scottish forces loyal to Charles II were defeated at the Battle of Dunbar in 1650. Parts of the castle were demolished to give Cromwell's troops a clear line of fire in the event that they should they come under attack.

During the Jacobite rebellion in 1746 William, Duke of Cumberland, arrived at Linlithgow, complete with 10,000 men. On their departure they left fires burning, which set the palace alight and left it roofless. Linlithgow never recovered from this accidental act of vandalism and today it is in the care of Historic Environment Scotland.

LEFT AND FAR LEFT The restored King's Fountain stands 5m (16ft) high and water cascades from the crown at the top. In 1745 it ran with wine to celebrate Bonnie Prince Charlie's arrival.

HUNTLY CASTLE, ABERDEENSHIRE

The grand ruins of Huntly Castle lie in Aberdeenshire and highlight the pleasures and perils of royal patronage. In 1190, King William of Scotland (1143–1214) granted Duncan, Earl of Fife, land in Strathbogie. By way of thanks Duncan was expected to secure the road here for the Crown. A motte and bailey castle, dubbed the Peel of Strathbogie, was constructed, but in the early 14th century King Robert I (1274–1329), popularly known as Robert the Bruce, gave the Strathbogie estate to one Alexander Gordon of Huntly, after Duncan IV, Earl of Fife, was suspected of supporting the English in the momentous Battle of Bannockburn (1314).

The Gordon family had extensive estates in southern Scotland and played an active part in battles to hold the Scottish border. So many died in the border struggles that by 1408, the male line was extinguished. Strathbogie passed via the female line through marriage to Sir Alexander Seton, Lord Gordon. To fit his newly elevated status Sir Alexander constructed an L-shaped tower house within the existing bailey.

A power struggle developing between the crown and the powerful Earls of Douglas was to impact Huntly Castle. In 1440, the ten-year-old King James II invited the 16-year-old William Douglas, the 6th Earl, along with his younger brother to dine in an event that became known as the Black Dinner. During the meal a black bulls head, a symbol of death, was brought in and placed before the Douglas brothers, who were then dragged outside, given a mock trial and executed. After centuries of royal fealty this brutal act motivated the Earls of Douglas to challenge the authority of the crown.

At the Peel of Strathbogie, Alexander Gordon (Alexander Seton's son who had reclaimed the old family name), supported the royal struggle against the Douglas clan, and in 1445 was created Earl of Huntly. A piqued Archibald Douglas, Earl of Moray, attacked Strathbogie in 1452 and burned the castle. This action further motivated the Earl of Huntly to move against the Douglas clan, and after a seven-year struggle their northern strongholds were defeated. In 1455 the Earl of Huntly set about reconstruction, building a great castle, and his son George Gordon, 2nd Earl of Huntly, continued the work after his father's death in 1470.

In 1506 the Peel of Strathbogie was renamed Huntly Castle by royal charter. George Gordon, 4th Earl of Huntly, became Chancellor in 1546 and rebuilt the castle, adding the round tower and turning the castle into a palace. In 1556 he hosted such a spectacular reception for Mary of Guise, the Queen Regent, that she was advised by the French ambassador to 'clip his wings'. In 1560 Mary Queen of Scots transferred the Earldom of Moray, which had been given to George in 1549, to her half-brother Lord James Stewart. The 4th Earl retreated to his estates and withdrew his support and was defeated at the Battle of Corrichie in 1562. He died of apoplexy after the battle and his son John Gordon was executed.

In 1569 the Castle was restored to George Gordon the 5th Earl; he died eight years later after a game of football. In 1594, George Gordon the 6th Earl, a lively character who had apparently learned nothing from his forbears, joined with the Earl of Errol in a Catholic revolt against James VI of Scotland. By way of response the King instructed that Huntly Castle should be

RIGHT A view of Huntly Castle from the courtyard.

'slighted': a report from the day stated, 'nothing was left unhocked savinge the greate olde tower which shall be blown up with powder'.

Incredibly, what was left of the castle was restored to the 6th Earl of Huntly in 1597, and just two years later relations with the crown were sufficiently recovered for him to be made 1st Marquis of Huntly. Repairs were commissioned, and the design was further embellished with the addition of oriel windows and carvings declaring allegiance to James VI and God. This view later saw the family become involved in a long struggle with the Covenantors who opposed the interference of Charles I in their country's religion.

George, Gordon, 2nd Marquess of Huntly (1592–1649) had spent much of his early life in England and was educated at court with Prince Charles, the future king. From 1638, for the next 11 years, he opposed the Covenantors. Huntly Castle was taken by General Munro and occupied by a garrison of his men. The 2nd Marquis alternately negotiated, led armies of men in the King's name, went into hiding and was finally captured and then beheaded on 22 March 1649. This marks the end of the Gordon family's residence at Huntly Castle, though it remained in their ownership. In 1752 the widow of the 3rd Duke of Gordon used stone from the castle ruins to build Huntly Lodge nearby.

In 1924 Huntly Castle was taken into the care of the state, and it is now under the guardianship of Historic Environment Scotland.

RIGHT Formerly known as the Peel of Strathbogie, Huntly Castle was reconstructed in 1455 after it was set alight in a tussle between opposing families.

RIGHT Cardoness Castle was destroyed by a violent feud between owner and former owner.

CARDONESS CASTLE, KIRKCUDBRIGHTSHIRE

Despite its name, Cardoness Castle is not a castle at all, but a tower house. Its history is coloured by the fate of its owners who were caught up in a cautionary tale of greed and violence.

Cardoness Castle, an early form of fortified accommodation, was constructed by James McCulloch *c.*1475. It sits proudly on a rocky ridge near the estuary of the River Fleet in southern Scotland. Standing 17m (56ft) tall, it boasts four storeys, all linked by a single spiral staircase, and cellars. The main hall, complete with stone fireplaces, cupboards and window seats, was on the first floor; further family accommodation lay above. The walls at the base are 3m (10ft) thick and there is a single entrance door. Gun loops enabled the inhabitants to take potshots at passers-by should the need arise. Prisoners were accommodated in the pit prison below the cellar.

The McCullochs seem to have been a lawless and litigious bunch. James McCulloch was five times involved in land tussles and married his daughter to a man he described as a 'natural idiot' in order to gain control of his land. James' son Ninian was tried for stealing 1,500 cattle from his own mother, while Sir Alexander McCulloch was twice tried for violence against his neighbours, who doubtless celebrated when he fell at the Battle of Flodden in 1513.

The constant squabbles with neighbours and resulting litigation forced the family to mortgage its estate, ultimately losing it to John Gordon in 1628. But the McCullochs were not ready to forfeit their lands so easily, and certainly not to the Gordons with whom they had a longstanding feud. Their persecution of the new inhabitants of Cardoness Castle was both colourful and protracted.

On the 19 August 1664, they entered the castle and pulled the ceiling down on the new Lady Cardoness, shooting her son William in the arm and hand. William, predicting that the McCullochs would return 'like a dog to its vomit', sensibly took his leave. His mother, who was made of sterner stuff remained and suffered the indignity of being tossed onto a dung heap, and on another occasion was forced to shelter from her attackers in the kitchen chimney. The Gordons took the matter to the authorities, and although the McCullochs were fined and sentenced to imprisonment for their lawless behaviour, no action was ever taken against them.

Matters came to a head on 6 October 1690 when Godfrey McCulloch visited William Gordon, supposedly concerning a dispute over cattle. He shot William again, this time in the knee, a wound that killed him a few hours later. On hearing this news McCulloch fled, reappearing a few years later living under an assumed name in Edinburgh. Here, on a visit to church in December 1696, he was spotted by one of his creditors who reputedly thundered: 'Shut the doors, there's a murderer in the house.' McCulloch was arrested, tried, sentenced to death, and beheaded on a Maiden, an early version of the guillotine at the Cross of Edinburgh on 26 March 1697.

The Gordons abandoned Cardoness Castle and it fell into ruin while the McCullochs fled to Ireland. Cardoness Castle was put under state care in 1927 and is now protected by Historic Environment Scotland.

PLACES TO VISIT

SOUTH WEST

Glastonbury Abbey
Abbey Gatehouse
Magdalene Street
Glastonbury
Somerset
BA6 9EL
+44 (0)1458 832267
info@glastonburyabbey.com
www.glastonburyabbey.com

East Pool Mine
Pool, near Redruth
Cornwall
TR15 3NP
+44 (0)1209 315027
eastpool@nationaltrust.org.uk
www.nationaltrust.org.uk/
    east-pool-mine

Botallack Mine
On the Tin Coast,
near St Just
Cornwall
+44 (0)1736 786004
botallack@nationaltrust.org.uk
www.nationaltrust.org.uk/botallack

Corfe Castle
The Square
Corfe Castle
Wareham
Dorset
BH20 5EZ
+44 (0)1929 481294
corfecastle@nationaltrust.org.uk
www.nationaltrust.org.uk/corfe-castle

Tintagel Castle
Castle Road
Tintagel
Cornwall
PL34 0HE
+44 (0)1840 770328
www.english-heritage.org.uk/
    visit/places/tintagel-castle/

Tyneham Village
MOD Ranges
East Lulworth
Wareham
Dorset
BH20 5QF
+44 (0)1929 404819
www.dorsetforyou.gov.uk/
    lulworth-range-walks

Stonehenge
Near Amesbury
Wiltshire
SP4 7DE
+44 (0)3703 331181
www.english-heritage.org.uk/
    visit/places/stonehenge/

SOUTH EAST AND EAST

Scotney Castle
Lamberhurst
Tunbridge Wells
Kent
TN3 8JN
+44 (0)1892 893820
scotneycastle@nationaltrust.org.uk
www.nationaltrust.org.uk/
    scotney-castle

Rochester Castle
Kent
ME1 1SW
+44 (0)1634 335882
https://www.english-heritage.org.uk/
    visit/places/rochester-castle/

Bodiam castle
Bodiam
near Robertsbridge
East Sussex
TN32 5UA
+44 (0)1580 830196
bodiamcastle@nationaltrust.org.uk
www.nationaltrust.org.uk/
    bodiam-castle

Maunsell Forts
Boat trips run from the South-East
coast to the Maunsell Forts from May
to September and should be booked
in advance. Please check the websites
below for further information:
X-Pilot is a former service vessel from
Gravesend that once piloted large
ships up the Thames. Trips sail from
All Tide Landing, Queensborough,
Isle of Sheppy, Kent.
www.x-pilot.co.uk
The Greta is a Thames sailing barge
that took part in the Dunkirk
evacuation in 1940. Trips sail from
Whitstable, Kent.
www.greta1892.co.uk
Project Redsands works to conserve
and preserve Redsands Fort.
www.project-redsand.com

Racton Monument
Stoughton
Chichester
West Sussex
PO18

Portchester Castle
Church Road
Portchester
Hampshire
PO16 9QW
+44 (0)2392 378291
https://www.english-heritage.org.uk/
    visit/places/portchester-castle/

Nymans
Handcross
near Haywards Heath
West Sussex
RH17 6EB
+44(0)1444 405250
nymans@nationaltrust.org.uk
www.nationaltrust.org.uk/nymans

Orford Ness
Orford
Woodbridge
Suffolk
+44 (0)1728 648024
orfordness@nationaltrust.org.uk
www.nationaltrust.org.uk/
    orford-ness-national-nature-reserve

The Gothic Tower
Wimpole Estate
Arrington
Royston
Cambridgeshire
SG8 0BW
+44 (0)1223 206000
wimpolehall@nationaltrust.org.uk
www.nationaltrust.org.uk/
wimpole-estate/features/wimpoles-
award-winning-gothic-tower-

MIDLANDS AND THE NORTH

Witley Court
Worcester Road
Great Witley
Worcestershire
WR6 6JT
+44 (0)1299 896636
www.english-heritage.org.uk/visit/
places/witley-court-and-gardens/

Lyveden New Bield
near Oundle
Northamptonshire
PE8 5AT
+44 (0)1832 205158
lyveden@nationaltrust.org.uk
www.nationaltrust.org.uk/lyveden

Kirby Hall
Off Kirby Lane
Corby
Northamptonshire
NN17 3EN
+44 (0)1536 203230
www.english-heritage.org.uk/
visit/places/kirby-hall/

Rievaulx Abbey
Rievaulx
Nr Helmsley
North Yorkshire
YO62 5LB
+44 (0)1439 798228
www.english-heritage.org.uk/
visit/places/rievaulx-abbey/

Fountains Abbey
Fountains
Ripon
North Yorkshire
HG4 3DY
+44 (0)1765 608888
fountainsabbey@nationaltrust.org.uk
www.nationaltrust.org.uk/
fountains-abbey-and-
studley-royal-water-garden

Whitby Abbey
Abbey Lane
Whitby
North Yorkshire
YO22 4JT
+44 (0)1947 603568
www.english-heritage.org.uk/
visit/places/whitby-abbey/

Hadrian's Wall (Housesteads Fort)
Near Bardon Mill
Hexham
Northumberland
NE47 6NN
+44 (0)1434 344525
housesteads@nationaltrust.org.uk
www.nationaltrust.org.uk/
hadrians-wall-and-housesteads-fort

Dunstanburgh Castle
Craster
Alnwick
Northumberland
NE66 3TT
+44 (0)1665 576231
dunstanburghcastle@
nationaltrust.org.uk
www.nationaltrust.org.uk/
dunstanburgh-castle

Brougham Castle
Moor Lane
Penrith
Cumbria
CA10 2AA
+44 (0)1768 862488
www.english-heritage.org.uk/
visit/places/brougham-castle/

Lowther Castle
Penrith
Cumbria
CA10 2HH
+44 (0)1931 712192
info@lowthercastle.org
www.lowthercastle.org/

Harewood Castle
Harewood
Leeds
LS17 9LG
+44 (0)113 218 1010
info@harewood.org
https://harewood.org/

WALES

Tintern Abbey
Tintern
NP16 6SE
+44 (0)1291 689251
tinternabbey@gov.wales
cadw.gov.wales/daysout/tinternabbey/

Pont Y Pandy Slate Mill
The ruins of Pont y Pandy slate mill
are found in the Cymystradllyn Valley.
Follow the A487 heading west from
Porthmadog, as you come out of
Penmorfa turn right and follow the
road and you will see the slate mill
on your left-hand side.
OS Grid Ref: SH54980 43296,
listed as Ynys-y-pandy
OS Explorer Map 18: Harlech,
Porthmadog & Bala/Y Bala

Dolaucothi Gold Mines
Pumsaint
Llanwrda
Carmarthenshire
SA19 8US
+44 (0)1558 650177
dolaucothi@nationaltrust.org.uk
www.nationaltrust.org.uk/
dolaucothi-gold-mines

Caerphilly Castle
Castle Street
Caerphilly
CF83 1JD
+44 (0)2920 883143
CaerphillyCastle@gov.wales
cadw.gov.wales/daysout/
caerphilly-castle/

Carreg Cennen Castle
Trapp
Llandeilo
SA19 6UA
+44 (0)1558 822291
cadw.gov.wales/daysout/
    Carreg-cennen-castle/

Beaumaris Castle
Castle Street
Beaumaris
LL58 8AP
+44 (0)1248 810361
beaumariscastle@gov.wales
cadw.gov.wales/daysout/
    beaumaris-castle/

NORTHERN IRELAND

Grey Abbey
Grey Abbey House,
Greyabbey Estate Office,
Newtownards,
County Down,
Northern Ireland,
BT22 2QA
+44 (0)2842 788666
office@greyabbeyestates.com
www.greyabbeyhouse.com/

Old Castle Crom
National Trust Crom Estate
Upper Lough Erne
Newtownbutler
County Fermanagh
BT92 8AJ
+44 (0)2867 738118
crom@nationaltrust.org.uk
www.nationaltrust.org.uk/crom

Downhill Demesne
Mussenden Road
Castlerock
County Londonderry
BT51 4RP
+44 (0)2870 848728
downhilldemesne@
    nationaltrust.org.uk
www.nationaltrust.org.uk/
    downhill-demesne-and-
    hezlett-house

SCOTLAND

Melrose Abbey
Abbey Street
Melrose
Roxburghshire
TD6 9LG
+44 (0)1896 822562
www.historicenvironment.scot/
    visit-a-place/places/melrose-abbey/

Skara Brae
Sandwick
Orkney
KW16 3LR
+44 (0)1856 841815
www.historicenvironment.scot/
    visit-a-place/places/skara-brae/

Sweetheart Abbey
New Abbey
Dumfries
DG2 8BU
+44 (0)1387 850397
www.historicenvironment.scot/
    visit-a-place/places/
    sweetheart-abbey/

Linlithgow Palace
Kirkgate
Linlithgow
West Lothian
EH49 7AL
+44 (0)1506 842896
www.historicenvironment.scot/
    visit-a-place/places/
    linlithgow-palace/

Huntly Castle
Castle Avenue
Huntly
AB54 4SH
+44 (0)1466 793191
www.historicenvironment.scot/
    visit-a-place/places/huntly-castle/

Cardoness Castle
Gatehouse of Fleet
Castle Douglas
Kirkcudbrightshire
DG7 2EH
+44 (0)1557 814427
www.historicenvironment.scot/
    visit-a-place/places/cardoness-castle/

INDEX

PICTURE CREDITS AND ACKNOWLEDGEMENTS

This book has been a delight to write from start to finish, and I have revelled in exploring ruins across the country, I am therefore indebted to my publisher Peter Taylor at Pavilion for giving me this opportunity. I must also thank Katie Bond and Amy Feldman at the National Trust. In addition, I am eternally grateful to my editor Kristy Richardson, my copy editor Katie Hewett, the splendid designers Tokiko Morishima and Ginny Zeal, and to Polly Powell for her faith in me.

This book would not have been possible without the assistance of the National Trust, the National Trust for Scotland, Historic Environment Scotland, Cadw, English Heritage, and assorted other heritage organisations whose local guides were a mine of information. Between them they patiently answered my many queries. They are too numerous to name individually, but I thank them for the enthusiasm and generosity with which they pass on their knowledge.

Finally I have to acknowledge the support and encouragement given by my family; my husband Eric, and children Florence and Teddy. They have put up with much benign neglect, an empty refrigerator and more ready meals than I care to admit while I put domestic life on hold to finish this book. My friend Sarah Gristwood can always be relied upon to produce a superb piece of research material, and my dear chums Fiona Lovering and Jill Alkin who always lift my spirits. Thank you one and all.